Jonathan Goodman is best known as a crime historian (he has been described by Jacques Barzun as 'the greatest living master of the true-crime literature' and by Julian Symons as 'the premier investigator of crimes past'), but he has also published novels, poetry, and articles on diverse non-criminous subjects, and has had a number of plays produced. He was for several years a theatre director and television producer, and is a frequent broadcaster. He is one of the few lay members of the British Academy of Forensic Sciences, a member of the Medico-Legal Society, and a member – and of the committee – of Our Society, sometimes called the 'Crimes Club'.

ACTS OF MURDER

Jonathan Goodman

FOREWORD BY
Richard Briers

Futura

A **Futura** Book

Copyright © Jonathan Goodman 1986

First published in Great Britain in 1986 by
Harrap Limited, London

This edition published in 1987 by
Futura Publications, a Division of
Macdonald & Co (Publishers) Ltd
London & Sydney
Reprinted 1987

ISBN 0 7088 3603 8

Photoset in Garamond by 🅣 Tek Art Limited, Croydon
Printed and bound in Great Britain by
The Guernsey Press Co. Ltd, Guernsey, Channel Islands
Futura Publications
A Division of
Macdonald & Co (Publishers) Ltd
Greater London House
Hampstead Road
London NW1 7QX

A member of Pergamon MCC Publishing Corporation plc

For Joan Miller,
who *was* Edith Thompson in the
first stage production of
A Pin to See the Peepshow
based on the Bywaters-Thompson murder case.

Programme

Foreword

Who remembers the actor William Terriss? Hardly
anyone, I reckon. Yet in the theatre of the 1890s, he
was as famous, as idolized, as a pop star is today.
Dashingly handsome, virile and humorous, he served
only a brief apprenticeship before being invited by the
'master of masters', Sir Henry Irving, to join him and
the incomparable Ellen Terry at the Lyceum Theatre,
where he became a favourite with the public and the
company.

He was the only young actor who could get round
Irving even when he was late for rehearsal, an
unforgivable sin in those days, and went so far as to
request that he be allowed a small share of Irving's
special limelight in a duel they fought in *The Corsican
Brothers:* 'Don't you think, Guv'nor, a few rays of the
moon might fall on me? – it shines equally, y'know, on
the just and the unjust.' Instead of a steely look and a
severe reprimand for such cheek, the great man was
amused and from then on shared his moonlight with
William!

Having grown in stature as an actor under Irving's
guidance during many happy seasons at the Lyceum,
he left to take command of the Adelphi Theatre, and
became a star in his own right. Wealth and fame were
his. The Adelphi became known as 'Terriss's Theatre',
and the public flocked to see him.

Then, at the very height of his success, the unbelievable happened. One night, as he was about to enter the
theatre by his private stage-door, a small-part actor
emerged from the shadows and —

But no; I must not give the story away. It can be
found in this book, along with other 'Acts of Murder',

all rivetingly told by Jonathan Goodman, who deserves the grateful thanks of theatre-lovers, film-fans, and anyone outside those categories who enjoys reading true tales of murder and mystery.

Richard Briers

Beginners

Premeditatively, this book doesn't entirely embody its subject. Definitiveness, all very well for telephone directories and dictionaries, is usually excessive elsewhere.

There have been other murders and suspicious terminations with stage or screen associations. Perhaps I shall write about some of them another time. By then, I may have made up my mind whether or not assassination should be considered a kind of murder or a separate sort of crime that happens also to have death as its object; but if I have decided that assassination qualifies, I shall not feel obliged to write about the crime set in Ford's Theatre, Washington, for though it is literarily nice for a crime to have repercussions, they, I feel, should be unpretentious, ripples merely, not waves that make their origin seem paltry.

The tales herein were seeded by articles I contributed to the *Manchester Evening News* at the invitation of that paper's senior assistant editor William Lloyd, and so I thank him before thanking alphabetical others: Ivan Butler; Nick Charlesworth; Peter Cotes; Major A. J. Dickinson, Secretary of the Royal Humane Society; Jack Hammond; Margaret Heppenstall; Richard Huggett; Peter Jackson (the illustration on page 25 is from his collection); Lucy Keddie; Thomas M. McDade; Alison McDougall; Daphne Phillips, Principal Librarian, Local Studies, at the Reading Central Library; Thomas Porter, General Manager of the Royal Adelphi Theatre from November 1951 till December 1984; George Raine, correspondent of *Newsweek*; Bill Waddell, Curator of the Crime Museum, New Scotland Yard, and Richard

Whittington-Egan.

The extracts from George Bernard Shaw's letters to Ellen Terry are reproduced by permission of The Society of Authors on behalf of the Bernard Shaw Estate.

Jonathan Goodman

The Death of the Devil's Disciple

Due to circumstances beyond anyone's control, the theatrical tradition that the show must go on was broken on 16 December 1897 at the Adelphi Theatre, London, where William Terriss, the most idolized of matinée idols, was starring as Captain Thorne, alias Lewis Dumont, in an American melodrama called *Secret Service*.[1]

The play was utter hokum (Bernard Shaw, reviewing the first production, had pointed to any number of

1. By the actor William Gillette. The play was first presented in London by an American cast headed by Gillette, and including Ethel Barrymore in a small role, on 15 May 1897; the production ran for three months. The revival starring William Terriss opened at the Adelphi on 24 November.

Gillette is best remembered as the author (with help from W. G. Postance) of the play *Sherlock Holmes*, mainly derived from Arthur Conan Doyle's tales, 'A Scandal in Bohemia' and 'The Final Problem'. He himself played the Master Detective in the original production, which opened at the Garrick Theatre, New York, on 6 November 1899, and in the first London production, at the Lyceum from 9 September 1901. While the play was still at the Lyceum, four companies were formed to take it round the provinces; the twelve-year-old Charles Chaplin played the part of Billy on one of the tours. Gillette continued to play Holmes – in the theatre, in a silent film and on radio – until 1935, two years before his death. Conan Doyle commented in his autobiography: 'Since [Gillette] used my characters and to some extent my plots, he naturally gave me a share in the undertaking, which proved to be very successful .... I was charmed both with the play, the acting and the pecuniary result.' *Sherlock Holmes* was successfully revived by the Royal Shakespeare Company at the Aldwych Theatre, London, on New Year's Day, 1974, with John Wood as Holmes and Philip Locke as Professor Moriarty.

incredible plot contrivances, noting in particular that 'before half an hour has elapsed the heroine quite forgets ... an act of fratricide on the part of the hero'); but still, the show was as great a hit as any of William Terriss's earlier ones at the Adelphi – a theatre that, though owned by the Italian restaurateurs, the Gatti brothers, had become known over the past several years as 'Terriss's domain'.

Terriss, whose real name was William Charles James Lewin, was born at St John's Wood, North London, in 1847. His father, a barrister, claimed kindredship with the Earl of Zetland; his mother was a niece of George Grote – so noted an historian of Greece that his remains were buried in Westminster Abbey and a bust of him placed in a proximate niche. At the age of seven, Terriss became a Bluecoat boy at Christ's Hospital; three or four years later, he moved to another school, then to another. He was already stage-struck; but, his parents refusing to countenance the idea of any son of theirs being a vulgar thespian, his first job was as a midshipman in the Royal Navy. While he was on leave in March 1865, an elderly aunt took him, wearing his uniform, to the Somerset seaside town of Weston-super-Mare. The visit had to be cut short because he was mistaken for Victoria and Albert's second son, Prince Arthur, Duke of Edinburgh, who was a lieutenant in the Navy, and attracted cheering and national-anthem-singing crowds wherever he went; according to a report in the *Bristol Times and Mirror*, the vicarious prince's smiling acceptance of the rowdy homage during his walkabouts greatly increased royalism in Weston. When William's aunt decided that they must leave and ordered a cab to take them to the railway station, the vehicle that eventually arrived was a beribboned carriage and pair, guided by postillions.

Receiving a small bequest on his eighteenth birthday, Terriss left the Royal Navy and took passage on a merchant vessel bound for Bengal, in north-western

India, where he meant to become a tea-planter. Owing to a shipwreck, the journey took longer than he had expected; on the other hand, he soon grew bored with planting tea at Chittagong, and so, after dabbling in the wine and tobacco trades in Calcutta, he returned to England within a few months of his departure. He tried banking, then went abroad again, this time to Louisiana, where he worked on a cotton plantation – briefly, because almost as soon as he arrived there, he decided that he had to be an actor. At New Orleans, he joined the crew of a cargo-ship that was collecting bales of cotton from Southern ports before sailing for Liverpool. He afterwards recalled that while scrubbing the deck, he dreamed of treading the boards.

In the summer of 1867 (he was now twenty), he found cheap digs in London and set about earning his living on the stage. Easier said than done. The theatrical profession was almost as overcrowded then as it is today; and there was no Actors' Equity Association to set minimum rates of pay. Terriss's first stage appearances – fleeting ones – were during a season of plays starring Madame Céleste at the Prince of Wales Theatre, Birmingham; he was paid eighteen shillings a week. Towards the end of 1868, he played a minor role in a London revival of T. W. Robertson's comedy *Society*. After two years – two years in which he was more often 'resting' than working, and in which the parts he did get were of the cough-and-a-spit variety – he came to the conclusion that an actor's life was not for him. However, he had one thing to be happy about: he had fallen in love with an actress named Amy Fellowes, and she had agreed to marry him – even though he had told her that he intended to emigrate to the Falkland Islands.

The young couple's honeymoon, if one can call it that, was spent on board a small ship travelling the 8,000 miles to the South Atlantic. Arriving at Port Stanley, they took a room at the Ship Hotel, and

Terriss at once began working from dawn till dusk as a sheep-breeder and tamer of wild horses. About a year later, in April 1871, Amy gave birth to a daughter, named Ellaline.

The child was only a couple of months old when her parents decided to return to England. The reason for the decision is not clear: it may be that William and Amy had simply grown tired of eking out a meagre existence in the bleak Falklands ... or perhaps William's yearning for a stage career had become strong again, to the extent that, when recalling his first attempt, the many periods of despair were misted in his memory, while the few good times were dazzlingly lime-lit.

In any event, on the very first day he got back to London, he bought a copy of a theatrical newspaper, scanned the audition advertisements and the reports of shows that were being cast, and then started a tour of producers' offices. A short tour, as it turned out. After making only a few calls, he found himself in the right place at the right time. A producer seeking a young (and inexpensive) actor took one look at Terriss, and was so impressed by his handsome face and fine physique – both attributes enhanced by the stay in the Falklands – that he engaged him on the spot for a show that was just going into rehearsal. When the play opened, Terriss received excellent notices; talent-spotters for other producers admired his gusto and charm: his name spread through the theatrical grape-vine.

Before the end of the run, he had offers of parts in forthcoming productions. He was able to pick and choose. And, with advice from Amy, he chose well, resisting the temptation to accept the highest-paid job, and instead taking a part that truly suited him. So it went on. In a remarkably short time – a matter of a year or so, for in those days any production that notched up more than a hundred performances was reckoned to have had a long run – William Terriss was being talked of as a rising star. Subsequently, a reporter for the stage weekly, *The Era*, noted:

During an extended engagement at the Strand Theatre in 1873–4, Mr Terriss played Doricourt, in *The Belle's Strategem*,[1] 250 times, winning golden opinions. He was then in the Drury Lane production of *Richard Coeur De Lion*,[2] playing Sir Kenneth. On the withdrawal of this play, Mr Terriss apppeared as Romeo to the Juliet of Miss Wallis, and when in September, 1875, *The Shaughraun* was produced, Mr Terriss was the Molyneux, both Dion[3] and Mrs Boucicault appearing in the production. Mr Terriss's Moly-neux suggested to the late Henry S. Leigh a charming set of verses, in which a pretty miss from the country, seeing Molyneux from her seat in the pit, is moved to a pretty confession of love for the handsome officer and jealousy of fortun-ate Claire. *The Shaughraun* was transferred to the Adelphi, and with it Mr Terriss. Here, and at the Princess's, he appeared in several revivals.

Terriss's really big chance came in March 1878, when he played opposite Ellen Terry, the most distinguished member of the famous theatrical family that is still represented in the person of John Gielgud (Ellen Terry's great-nephew).

Terry … Terriss. The similarity between the names must have caused confusion to some readers of the

1. The Restoration-style comedy by Hannah Cowley, first produced in 1780 at Covent Garden.

2. Adapted by James Burgoyne from a French romance; first produced in 1786 at Drury Lane.

3. Not to be confused with his same-named and even more successful son.

playbill. More to the point of this story, the similarity
would create a motive for murder.

The play, presented by the actor-manager John
Hare, was *Olivia*, an adaptation of Goldsmith's *The
Vicar of Wakefield* by W. G. Wills (who was an
extraordinarily industrious turner of novels into plays;
a few years before, Terriss had played Julian Peveril in
a short-lived Drury Lane production of Wills's version
of Scott's *Peveril of the Peak*). In *The Story of My Life*
(published in 1908), Ellen Terry remembered that:

> ... like all Hare's plays, *Olivia* was perfectly cast.
> Where all were good, it will be admitted, I think,
> by everyone who saw the production, that Terriss
> was the best. 'As you stand there, whipping your
> boot, you look the very picture of vain indiffer-
> ence,' Olivia says to Squire Thornhill in the first
> act, and never did I say it without thinking how
> absolutely *to the life* Terriss realized that descrip-
> tion!
>
> As I look back, I remember no figure in the
> theatre more remarkable than Terriss. He was one
> of those heaven-born actors who, like kings by
> divine right, can, up to a certain point, do no
> wrong. Very often, like Dr Johnson's 'inspired
> idiot', Mrs Pritchard, he did not know what he
> was talking about. Yet he 'got there', while many
> cleverer men stayed behind. He had unbounded
> impudence, yet so much charm that no one could
> ever be angry with him. Sometimes he reminded
> me of a butcher-boy flashing past, whistling, on
> the high seat of his cart, or of Phaethon driving
> the chariot of the sun – pretty much the same
> thing, I imagine! When he was 'dressed up',
> Terriss was spoiled by fine feathers; when he was
> in rough clothes, he looked like a prince. He
> always commanded the love of his intimates as
> well as that of the outside public. To the end he

was 'Sailor Bill' – a sort of grown-up midship-mite, whose weaknesses provoked no more condemnation than the weaknesses of a child ....

Terriss had had every sort of adventure by land and sea before I acted with him at the Court Theatre .... He had, to use his own words, 'hobnobbed with every kind of queer folk, and found himself in extremely queer predicaments'. The adventurous, dare-devil spirit of the roamer, the incarnate gipsy, always looked out of his insolent eyes. Yet, audacious as he seemed, no man was ever more nervous on the stage. On a first night he was shaking all over with fright, in spite of his confident and dashing appearance ....

When he had presents from the front, which happened every night, he gave them at once to the call-boy or the gas-man. To the women-folk, especially the plainer ones, he was always delightful. Never was any man more adored by the theatre staff. And children, my own Edy included, were simply *daft* about him. A little American girl, daughter of William Winter, the famous critic, when staying with me in England, announced gravely when we were out driving:

'I've gone a mash on Terriss.'

There was much laughter. When it had subsided, the child said gravely:

'Oh, you can laugh, but it's true. I wish I was hammered to him!'

... His conversation was extremely entertaining – and, let me add, ingenuous. One of his favourite reflections was:

'Tempus fugit! So make the most of it. While you're alive, gather roses; for when you're dead, you're dead a d----d long time.'

Soon after Ellen Terry's first appearance with Terriss, she became the leading lady of Henry Irving's company at the Lyceum. Terriss accepted an engagement at the Haymarket, where he played a number of leading roles, including that of Captain Absolute in *The Rivals*, and then, in the winter of 1879, rejoined John Hare for a season at the St James's.

In 1880, seemingly at Ellen Terry's insistence, Henry Irving invited Terriss to join the Lyceum company to play the villain, Château-Renaud, in a revival of *The Corsican Brothers* (adapted from the French by Dion Boucicault). Terriss stayed with the company for five years, appearing most notably as Cassio in the production of *Othello* (May 1881) in which Irving and the American actor Edwin Booth (an elder brother of John Wilkes Booth, assassinator of Lincoln) alternated as Othello and Iago; as Mercutio to Irving's Romeo and Ellen Terry's Juliet (most critics felt that the production would have been improved if Irving and Terriss had swapped roles; a play-going politician commented, 'As Romeo, Irving reminds me of a pig who has been taught to play the fiddle. He does it cleverly, but he would be better employed in squealing. He cannot shine in the part like the fiddler. Terriss in this case is the fiddler'); as Don Pedro in the production of *Much Ado About Nothing* which the dramatist Arthur Wing Pinero considered 'as perfect a representation of a Shakespearian play as is possible' (the production ran for 212 performances, and would have continued but for the fact that arrangements had been made for the company, including Terriss, to tour America, starting in the autumn of 1883).

In her autobiography, Ellen Terry cited Terriss's performance as Don Pedro to support her conviction that, when playing Shakespeare, 'he often did not know what he was talking about':

> One morning [during rehearsals] we went over
> and over one scene in 'Much Ado' – at least a
> dozen times, I should think – and each time when

Terriss came to the speech beginning: 'What needs the bridge much broader than the flood,' he managed to give a different emphasis. First it would be:

'What! Needs the bridge much broader than the flood.' Then:

'What needs the bridge *much* broader than the flood.'

After he had been floundering about for some time, Henry said:

'Terriss, what's the meaning of that?'

'Oh, get along, Guv'nor, *you* know!'

Henry laughed. He never could be angry with Terriss, not even when he came to rehearsal full of absurd excuses. One day, however, he was so late that it was past a joke, and Henry spoke to him sharply.

'I think you'll be sorry you've spoken to me like this, Guv'nor,' said Terriss, casting down his eyes.

'Now no hanky-panky tricks, Terriss.'

'Tricks, Guv'nor! I think you'll regret having said that when you hear that my poor mother passed away early this morning.'

And Terriss wept.

Henry promptly gave him the day off. A few weeks later, when Terriss and I were looking through the curtain at the audience just before the play began, he said to me gaily:

'See that dear old woman sitting in the fourth row of the stalls – that's my dear old mother.'

The wretch had quite forgotten that he had killed her!

He was the only person who ever ventured to 'cheek' Henry, yet he never gave offence, not even when he wrote a letter of this kind:

'My Dear Guv.,

'I hope you are enjoying yourself, and in the best of health. I very much want to play 'Othello' with you next year (don't laugh). Shall I study it up, and will you do it with me on tour if possible? Say *yes*, and lighten the drooping heart of yours sincerely,

'WILL TERRISS.'

I have never seen anyone at all like Terriss .... One night he came into the theatre soaked from head to foot.

'Is it raining, Terriss?' said someone who noticed that he was wet.

'Looks like it, doesn't it?' said Terriss carelessly.

Later it came out that he had jumped off a penny steamboat into the Thames and saved a little girl's life. It was pretty brave, I think.[1]

Terriss left the Lyceum at Christmas 1885; the company gave him a silver loving cup, but he treasured more the gift of a gold-mounted riding whip from the stage-hands. During the following three years, he starred in a string of melodramas at the Adelphi

---

1. Terriss was less modest about another brave deed, going in person to the Royal Humane Society's office, which was then in Trafalgar Square, to report it.

In the early evening of 6 August 1885, he and a companion were sailing off South Foreland, near the town of Deal, in Kent, when one of three boys who were swimming nearby developed cramp. Terriss lowered his lugsail, jumped overboard fully clothed, and kept the boy afloat till the other yachtsman had thrown a line and hauled him to safety.

The Royal Humane Society decided that Terriss's act merited the award of a Bronze Medal. Having recovered his modesty, he was absent from the Lyceum on 29 September, when a representative of the Society called to present him with the medal, and so it was accepted on his behalf by Henry Irving.

Theatre in the Strand, just round the corner from the Lyceum: *The Harbour Lights, The Bells of Haslemere, The Union Jack,* and – lastly, opening on 29 December 1888 – *The Silver Falls.* In most of these productions, the female lead was played by the strikingly beautiful actress, Miss [Jessie] Millward, whom Terriss had enticed from Irving. Naturally, and perhaps with some foundation, there was tittle-tattle that the stage love-scenes between Terriss and Miss Millward were inst-ances of art imitating nature; tongues continued to wag, and the tongue-waggers tended to be more reckless with rumour, when, for some eight months from the autumn of 1889, the couple toured America, most often playing the Haymarket success *A Man's Shadow* (which for some reason was billed as *Roger La Honte* in the States).

After his first American tour, with Irving and Ellen Terry, Terriss had been instrumental in arranging for Augustin Daly's company to visit England. As soon as he returned from the second tour, he went into partnership with Sir Augustus Harris to present an American drama called *Paul Kauvar* at Drury Lane; without his presence in the cast, the production was a costly failure (as was another American play, *The Great Metropolis*, which he, having helped in its anglicization, put on at the Princess's two years later). Straightway, he rejoined the Lyceum company; and remained with it for about two years, playing Hayston of Bucklaw in *Ravenswood*, Herman Merivale's adap-tation of Scott's *The Bride of Lammermoor*, the respective Kings in *Henry VIII* and *Becket*,[1] and the eponymous hero of W. G. Wills's adaptation of Goethe's *Faust*.

In the summer of 1894, Terriss accepted the Gatti

1. Lord Tennyson's play, arranged for the stage by Irving – who died after playing the title-role at Bradford on 13 October 1905. (Ten years before, he had become the first actor-knight.)

brothers' invitation to star in melodramas of his choosing at the Adelphi. The project was successful from the start (that being on 6 September, with a production of *The Fatal Card*); the House-Full board was more often on display before the curtain went up than was the Standing-Room-Only one for shows like *The Girl I Left Behind Me* (almost as great a hit in the West End as it had been, natively, in New York), *The Swordsman's Daughter* (by Clement Scott, the Ibsen-loathing drama critic of the *Daily Telegraph*, and Brandon Thomas, whose *Charley's Aunt* had first appeared in London in 1892), and *One of the Best* (which Shaw reviewed under the heading of 'One of the Worst'; it was written by George Edwardes, manager of the Gaiety Theatre, at the eastern end of the Strand, and the young comedy-actor Seymour Hicks, husband of Terriss's daughter Ellaline, who had begun her own stage career in 1888, when she was sixteen). Terriss, always the hero, rescued distressed damsels (usually depicted by Jessie Millward), foiled dastardly villains, and declaimed yard-long speeches about chivalry, honour, and suchlike.

He became known to the public by several affection-ate sobriquets: 'Sailor Bill' was one, 'Breezy Bill' another. People who had never met him felt that they knew him well; they would wave to him in the street – and he would wave back. There was nothing false about his affability. He had a wide circle of friends, not just stage-people, and on Sundays he and Amy often gave parties at their house – far grander than its name of The Cottage suggested – in Bedford Road, Turnham Green, on the western hem of London. Years later, a journalist who presumably had visited The Cottage wrote:

> Some of Mr Terriss's happiest hours were spent at his pretty house. The home life of the hero of so many melodramas was a model of comfort and

good taste. Ferns and flowers, music and art, pleasant society, long rides upon a favourite mare, lawn tennis and quoits, much smoking and more reading went to make up the daily round from year's end to year's end. Picture-books, curios in every corner of the house, evidenced the artistic feeling of its tenant. Mr Terriss … welcomed his pleasant and quiet life in Turnham Green after the artificial surroundings of the stage, the more so, perhaps, that his earlier years were full of stir and vicissitude.

Terriss, as well as owning The Cottage, leased an apartment in Princes Street, off Hanover Square. On week-days, if he was not rehearsing or playing, he could usually be found either at the apartment or at the Green Room Club in Bedford Street, close to the Adelphi Theatre. Perhaps because he didn't relish travelling the seven or so miles to Turnham Green after evening performances, which rarely ended much before eleven o'clock, he often slept at the apartment; gossip that he sometimes shared his bed with Jessie Millward seems to have started off as a guess from the fact that she also had an apartment in Princes Street, and flourished without the aid of evidence.

Either because he was innately kind or because of memories of his own adversities when he had started in the theatre, he was very generous towards members of his profession who were down on their luck. As well as donating to and appearing in charity matinées for the Actors' Benevolent Fund, the offices of which were in Adam Street, diagonally across the Strand from the Adelphi Theatre, he always listened sympathetically to hard-luck stories from actors with whom he had worked, and almost always gave them money.

One recipient of Terriss's hand-outs was a man called Richard Archer Prince, a native of Dundee who had acquired the nickname – never used to his face, of course – of 'Mad Archer'. He was short of stature, and his most conspicuous facial distinctions were a heavy black moustache with waxed tips, and a squinting left eye. The squinting doesn't seem to have diminished his belief that he was exquisitely good-looking, for he frequently bragged: 'I am a member of the handsomest family in Scotland.'

His stage appearances hardly entitled him to call the stage his career: subordinate roles in touring productions – from which he was often sacked for hamming or quite forgetting his one or two speeches – and non-speaking or one-line parts in London shows, so particularly at the Adelphi that he had calling-cards printed:

Mr Richard Archer Prince
Adelphi Theatre, Strand, London.

Since he sometimes used other names, and was sometimes denied acknowledgment in the programmes of shows in which he did little more than 'dress the set', it would not be possible, even if considered worthwhile, to make up a full catalogue of his slight contributions to productions in the West End. So far as the Adelphi is concerned, it seems that he first worked there in October 1880 (when he was twenty-two, just down from Dundee), playing the taciturn role of Sligo Dan in *The O'Dowd*, which was written by, and on this occasion starred, Dion Boucicault. Five months later, he was the First Traveller in *Michael Strogoff*, a drama adapted from the French by H. J. Byron,[1] and in the autumn of that same year, 1881, he was the Groom in a revival of Charles Reade's *It's Never Too Late To Mend*. From October 1883 – for more than a year, if he did not leave or was not replaced before the end of the

---

1. Author of many stage-offerings, the most lastingly influential being a burlesque, performed in the 1860s, from which the pantomime *Aladdin* is derived.

extremely successful run – he was O'Flanigan in the large cast of *In the Ranks* by the prolific collaborators George R. Sims and Henry Pettitt. Prince's ever-tenuous association with the Adelphi continued during William Terriss's first spell at the theatre, starting in December 1885; he was a supernumerary in a couple of the early productions, and had a little to say as Diego, one of half a dozen Miners, in the final play, *The Silver Falls*, which was also by Sims and Pettitt. It is likely that he played some small role in the penultimate production, of *The Union Jack* by Pettitt and Sydney Grundy – though not that of Tim O'Grady, the minor character he portrayed when the patriotic drama was taken on tour in 1889, at about the time that Terriss and Jessie Millward were embarking for America.

If Prince got any work at the Adelphi in the years between the closure of *The Silver Falls* and Terriss's return, his contribution was not such as to warrant being mentioned in a programme. There seems no doubt that he augmented crowds in at least two productions during Terriss's second spell at the theatre, but which productions these were is a matter for conjecture.

The longer 'Mad Archer' remained a failure as an actor, the more certain he became that he was God's gift to the stage. So as to keep his egotism intact, he *had* to assume that his signal lack of success was due to a conspiracy among the male stars: they feared that, if he were given the chance, he would outshine them. It was obvious, wasn't it? – well, *wasn't* it? – that the stars had noted, and been frightened by, the fact that though he had never been allowed to declaim anything more dramatic than 'the carriage awaits, m'lord', his ability to make a little go a long way caused audiences to gape and to gasp at the realization that they were glimpsing genius. The stars – all for one and one for all – were determined that he should never reign as the Prince of Players, showing up their second-rate talents.

During an engagement at the Adelphi, Prince's jealous hatred of the stars was turned into enmity against one in particular. The crowd-players in the communal dressing-room, sick and tired of his conceited chatter, pretended to agree that he, not William Terriss, should be playing the leading role in the play – and added that he *might* be were it not that Terriss had informed the Gatti brothers that he would walk out if Prince was given a speaking part. It never occurred to Prince that he was being 'sent up', and from then on he regarded Terriss as his implacable enemy.

Actually, Terriss felt sorry for Prince. On several of the occasions when Prince had applied to the Actors' Benevolent Fund for financial assistance, Terriss had spoken up for him; once, when the emergency committee had voted against providing help, he had given money to the secretary, Charles Coltson, to pass on to Prince.

In December of 1897, the year of Queen Victoria's diamond jubilee, both men, the matinée idol and the nonentity, were deeply disturbed.

William Terriss was worried about his daughter Ellaline, who at the end of November, undisguisably pregnant, had needed to leave the Gaiety, where for the past two and a half years she had been playing leading roles, usually opposite her husband Seymour Hicks, in George Edwardes's *Girl* series of musical comedies (*The Shop Girl, My Girl, The Circus Girl*). Following a miscarriage, she had spent a week or so in a rest-home at Eastbourne; but, her condition having deteriorated to the extent that she needed to fight for breath, she had been brought back to London to be admitted to the Charing Cross Hospital. There, the doctors expressed concern that she might not recover. Wanting to be with her as often as possible, Terriss had cancelled many daytime engagements, including activities associated with the Actors' Benevolent Fund.

Prince's worries were to do with finance – or rather,

his lack of it. Having been unemployed for months, he had pawned virtually all of his belongings apart from a single set of indoor clothes, a grey Inverness cloak and a black slouch-hat. He was in arrears with the four-shillings-a-week rent for his bed-sitter in the home of a bus-driver at 16 Ebury Court, near Victoria Station, and the only food he could afford was bread dipped in milk; the bus-driver's wife had threatened to turn him out, not just because he was behind with the rent but also because his small back room was 'like a pig-sty', littered with theatrical newspapers, religious tracts, and notices of services at Westminster Abbey.

Since 1890, Prince had occasionally received small sums, never more than a pound, from the Actors' Benevolent Fund, but from early in November 1897 he had become 'a weekly applicant for relief'. When making the first of the weekly applications, he had produced a note from William Terriss: 'I know the bearer, Richard A. Prince, as a hard-working actor.' Terriss's 'reference' had persuaded the emergency committee to grant Prince thirty shillings, and he had at once written to Charles Coltson:

Dear Sir,
    I don't know how to thank you and the gentlemen of the Committee for your great kindness. It's worth ten years of one's life to receive such favours from one in the poor position I have always had at my art. But I hope to Almighty God my luck will change in the week to pay back such kindness. Thanking you, Sir, for the way in which you have received me at the Actors' Benevolent Fund. You do it the greatest honour. If it's ever in my power, with the help of God, to do it any good, I will.
    Yours very faithfully,
    With thanks,
RICHARD A. PRINCE

Apart from the use of pale-violet ink, that communication was very different from one that Charles Coltson received on 4 December: a card, posted in Paddington at 12.15 a.m. that day. The sender's address began, '8 War St,' but then straggled into illegibility; though the message looked as if it had been dashed off, an attempt seemed to have been made to disguise the writing. The message read:

> I am coming up to town next week, and I shall wait on your coming out, and you will have to go through with it. Odd man out you will be. After next Monday shall kill you.
>
> Yours,
>
> FIND OUT

Mr Coltson – who was addressed as 'John Colman' on the card – was sure that the anonymous correspondent was Prince, who, only the day before, had made a scene in the Fund's offices after being told that his latest plea had resulted in an award of a mere five shillings.

Apparently, Mr Coltson did not worry about the threat. And he did not mention it when, on Wednesday, 15 December, Prince again turned up at the Fund's offices – only to be told that, for the time being, at any rate, he was to receive no further aid. Prince, who seemed to take the decision stoically, asked who had chaired the emergency committee that day. 'One of the Terrys,' he was told.

If Prince heard the first three words of that reply, he ignored them. It was a name that crowded his mind: not the plural 'Terrys' that had been spoken but the singular 'Terriss' that he had desperately wanted to hear. Once again, he had been victimized by the idol of the Adelphi.

As it happened, a few hours later William Terriss saw Prince in the street. He stopped to speak to him, and before saying good-luck and goodbye, pressed some money into his hand.

Prince spent part of the gift – one shilling and ninepence, to be exact – at a shop in Victoria Street which specialized in butchering equipment. His purchase was a filleting knife, its handle fashioned from red teakwood, its blade, of Sheffield steel, honed on both edges and dwindling to a needle-sharp point.

Thursday, 16 December 1897, was a cold but harshly bright day. The Strand was crowded with Christmas shoppers. And long before the box-office opened at the Adelphi Theatre, the foyer was jam-packed with people hoping to acquire the few remaining seats for that evening's performance of one of the biggest hits in town, the American melodrama *Secret Service*, starring William Terriss and – her name less prominent than his on the playbill – Miss Millward. By half-past ten or so, the House-Full board was being displayed.

The ticket holders, nigh on a thousand of them, would be disappointed, for the Adelphi's scarlet-and-gold curtain would not rise that evening. A few minutes after eight o'clock, when the performance was due to start, the slit in the centre of the curtain would be opened, and the assistant manager, George Budd, resplendent in tails but grey-faced and looking as if he had been crying, would make an announcement:

'Ladies and gentlemen, I am deeply grieved and pained to inform you that because of a serious – nay, terrible – accident, it is impossible for the performance of *Secret Service* to take place. I will ask you to be good enough to pass out into the street as quietly as possible. It is hardly necessary for me to add that your money will be returned on application at the pay-box.'

During the morning of that fateful Thursday, William Terriss, with his son-in-law Seymour Hicks, had visited his daughter Ellaline at the Charing Cross Hospital. By midday, he was back at his apartment in Princes Street, keeping an appointment with an old and elderly friend, a surveyor named John Graves, who was giving him advice, presumably on a business footing, concerning his intention to enlarge the fern-filled conservatory attached to his house in Turnham Green. In the early afternoon, he and Graves went by hansom-cab to the Green Room Club. Having lunched – Graves with gusto; Terriss, as was his custom, but lightly – they both took a nap in the library, a room with almost as many green-leather armchairs as books, and then joined in a game of nap with three other members of the club, one of whom was Herbert Waring, a rising actor whom some critics had compared to Terriss in terms of personableness and panache. Terriss was a keen gambler (Seymour Hicks subsequently recalled seeing him lose or win hundreds of pounds during an afternoon or late-night card-playing session); but this afternoon his mind was not on the game. Every so often, he would leave the table to make a telephone call to the hospital or to The Cottage.

As the brass clock chimed for 7.15, he finished off his pre-performance tumbler of whisky and water, donned his tweed overcoat and brown soft hat, and left for the theatre, intending to be in his dressing-room just in time to answer the call-boy's knock and shout of 'half an hour' at 7.25. He was accompanied by Graves – whose name would soon, very soon, be construed as ill-omened by superstitious stage-folk.

Graves had been one of Terriss's guests at the first night of *Secret Service*, and had afterwards complained to his friend that some members of the audience seemed to have come along more to be seen and heard than to see and hear. Now, strolling with Terriss down Bedford Street, he said that he hoped that tonight's audience, of which he would be a complimentary part, would be less participative than the first one. Terriss told Graves that, a few years before, a controversy about first-nighters had blown up in the correspondence columns of a stage paper, and he had put his spoke in, declaring that while he much preferred to be applauded, he freely admitted the right of first-nighters to hiss or otherwise indicate their displeasure. Recalling part of what he had written, he quoted it to Graves: 'It is all very well to claim the indulgence due to ladies and gentlemen, but artists should remember that they are actors and actresses when they are on the boards, and if they wish to be treated as ladies and gentlemen only, they had better remain in that privacy with which the public will not interfere, and where they will be free alike from public applause and public censure.' By the end of the recitation, the two men had turned left and were entering Maiden Lane; Terriss was feeling in his pocket for a silver key.

Little is known of how Richard Archer Prince spent the daylight hours and then the first hours of darkness of that Thursday. Subsequently, several people, most of them actors as derelict as Prince, claimed to have observed him walking – or, to stick to their words, 'lurching', 'shambling', or 'wandering sightlessly' – in different parts of the West End; none had spoken to him, and he had not spoken to any of them. In the morning, at about eleven o'clock, he was close to the Adelphi Theatre – on the other side of the Strand, in the offices of the Actors' Benevolent fund, where he pleaded with Charles Coltson for his case to be reconsidered and was told to come back next day, when the emergency committee would be meeting.

By seven in the evening, he was closer still to the Adelphi: standing in a shadowed side-doorway of Rule's Restaurant[1] in Maiden Lane, at the rear of the theatre.

---

1.   Still the second-oldest eating house in London; the oldest is the Cheshire Cheese, just to the east, off Fleet Street. Dr Thomas Neill Cream – graduate of M'Gill College, Montreal, 1876; poisoner of four Waterloo-based prostitutes, 1891–2; one of the many – too many – people blamed by Ripperologists for the Whitechapel Murders of 1888 (when, but never mind, he was in a Chicago prison, serving a life sentence for murder) – was a

The Adelphi had two stage-doors. Over the years since 1880, whenever Prince was working at the theatre, supernumerarily or with a couple of lines to speak, he had used the main stage-door, which was in Bull Inn Court, running down the eastern side of the building from Maiden Lane to the Strand. The other door, diagonally across from Rule's, was known as the Royal Entrance – more on account of the Sovereign's crest carved in stone above it than because it had occasionally been used by subjects-eschewing regal theatregoers. There were only two keys, both cut from silver, to this door; one was retained, but rarely used, by Arthur Latham, the manager of the theatre, and the other had been presented to William Terriss by the

regular customer at Rule's until 3 June 1892, when he was arrested, eventually to be charged with the murder of the aforementioned prostitutes. And, later, Dr Hawley Harvey Crippen (whose name will recur, set tall, in the piece called *Death in Carpet-Slippers*) patronized Rules, and became friendly with Harry Davis, who was then the manager. Long after Crippen's execution at Pentonville Prison in November 1910, Mr Davis was quoted as saying:

'I remember him well. The first time he came into Rule's he attracted my attention. There was about him an air, a something which I can't describe but which lifted him out of the common rut. He radiated vitality; there was a personal magnetism which drew other people to him ....

'I confess I found Crippen a charming companion. I and my wife often dined at his splendidly-appointed house, 39 Hilldrop Crescent, North London, and it was there I met his wife – a music-hall artist known professionally as Belle Elmore – "La Belle Americaine".

'Despite the fascination and charm of his wife, Crippen was not happy with her. Some mornings after particularly violent quarrels he would sit moodily over his drink, brooding, and despondent. Once, just before he committed the ghastly murder, he came into Rule's with scratches on his face.

'"I'm tired of it all, Harry," he said. "We've been fighting again; I don't know how it's going to end, but it certainly will. Another brandy."'

Gatti brothers, thus allowing him to treat the Royal Entrance virtually as his alone. Who knows? ... perhaps the fact that there were two doors – 'Gentleman' and 'Players' – aggravated Prince's jealous hatred of the star.

7.23

Cold from standing so long in the shadows, his hunger made painful by the sounds from the crowded restaurant – the customers' chatter, the clatter of crockery, the chinking of glasses – and by the smells wafting through the grille of the basement-kitchen, Prince slipped the brand-new filleting knife from the pocket of his cloak as, to his right, William Terriss and a man he did not know turned the corner from Bedford Street into Maiden Lane.

It seems likely that Terriss, quoting from a letter that he himself had written, spoke with more resonance than was his offstage wont; that Prince heard the end of what, because of his action, now just a few seconds away, would be Terriss's final sustained speech:

'*...free alike from public applause and public censure.*'

As Terriss inserted the key in the lock of the private door, Prince darted across the lane. He plunged the knife obliquely downwards into Terriss's back. Withdrew it. Struck again. If, preparing for the act, he had thought up something dramatic to exclaim – something impeccably iambic, short and to the points of explanation and exculpation – he quite forgot the line.

The only sound from Terriss – uttered twice – was a ragged expulsion of breath: 'not unlike the blowing-out of birthday candles', it seemed to John Graves, who, for the moment, felt no alarm. He 'thought that the strokes were merely hearty slaps, given in friendship'.

Still clutching the silver key, Terriss turned away from the door, staggered back against it. Did he have time to recognize his attacker? Probably not. As he

staggered – as he cried out: 'My God, I have ...' –
Princes rammed the knife into his breast.

'... been stabbed,' Terriss whispered. He fell untidily, his body jerking as he fell: a marionette whose
strings were being snipped one by one. Prince kept
hold of the knife; he did not let the falling body pull it
from his grasp, and as Terriss collapsed on the
pavement, the tarnished blade gradually slid back into
sight. Carefully, as if stowing a personal prop that
would be needed at further performances, Prince
replaced the knife in his pocket.

Graves stared at him, saw that he was smiling, and –
perhaps because inconsequential details tend to assume
a sham importance in times of stress – noticed that the
light filtering through the red gas-globe fixed to the
wall above the door gave an auburn tint to the waxed
tips of his moustache. Only afterwards did it occur to
Graves that it was odd that Terriss's attacker did not
run away. And then, one may surmise, he also
wondered at, and was quietly proud of, the courage he
himself showed by gripping Prince's arm and shouting,
not screaming, for help.

Among those who responded to Graves's shouts of
'Murder!', of 'Police!', was a member of the Corps of
Commissionaires who was making his way via the
back-doubles from his headquarters in the Strand to a
post office near Leicester Square. He broke into a run
and was the first to arrive; but rather than tendering
assistance to either Terriss or Graves, he stationed
himself in the middle of the lane, ready to exert his
uniformed authority in keeping spectators at bay. The
first of these emerged from Rule's – among them, a
journalist who the following morning would thrill
readers with his eye-witness account of the attack.

Inside the theatre, Terriss's dresser William Algar
dashed to the window of the first-floor dressing-room
to see what the commotion was about. Like the
journalist, he would profess to have seen the entire

THE LATE WILLIAM TERRISS

HOUSE WHERE PRISONER LIVED

MR TERRISS'S HOME . BEDFORD PARK .

OUL ASSASSINATION OF WILLIAM TERRISS, THE CELEBRATED ACTOR.
FROM DESCRIPTIONS BY EYE WITNESSES.

incident; but for the moment all he knew was that someone – it looked very much like his master – was spread-eagled on the ground, and two other men, one making all the noise, were standing close by, seemingly hand in hand. Just to be on the safe side, Algar grabbed a dress-sword, addendum to a costume that Terriss was due to wear on stage that night, before running out of the room and down the stone steps towards the Royal Entrance. His progress was sufficiently noisy to excite the attention of other dressers, of stage-hands; to bring actors and actresses, various in their preparation for the performance, from the dressing-rooms. And so he was one of several men who put their shoulders or hands to the door, forcing it wide and, in so doing, pushing William Terriss towards the gutter.

It was as if the scene had been rehearsed. The people from the theatre fanned out around the fallen star. Those nearest the door shuffled aside, letting Jessie Millward come through. She was wearing a many-coloured kimono, a present from Ellen Terry. For a moment she stared down at Terriss. Then, falling beside him, she cradled his head, lifted it towards her own. She was weeping now. Her tears glistened on Terriss's cheeks. With her free hand, she loosened the knot in his tie, tried to undo his collar.

But the tableau came to an unsatisfactory end. Terriss, hardly able to breathe, muttered, 'Get away ... get away.' An elderly woman – probably Mrs Briggs, the wardrobe mistress – pulled Jessie to her feet. Some stage-hands carried Terriss through the Royal Entrance and up the steps to his dressing-room. Blood dropped lavishly from him. Though he was barely conscious, he still gripped the silver key.

Before following, Jessie demonstrated that she was not so overcome that she was unable to behave sensibly. As well as sending the stage manager through to the stall-bar for ice, she despatched William Algar to the Charing Cross Hospital to fetch medical aid; and she told the call-boy to run to the Gaiety Theatre and inform Seymour Hicks, playing there in *The Circus Girl*, that his father-in-law had been seriously wounded. If she thought at all of Mrs Terriss, perhaps she decided that Hicks should break the news to her.

In the dressing-room, the death scene – for so it was – suffered, dramatically speaking, from the fact that the sofa of crimson velvet on which Terriss had been lain was shorter than his body, thus necessitating an unartistic lolling of his legs over an end; and from the fact that he was too far gone to speak dying words.

Down in the lane, it seemed that Richard Archer Prince had muffed his big chance of a sort of stardom. He had cast himself in the leading role of Murderer, but failed to impress anyone other than John Graves, who was still clutching his sleeve. By the time Police Constable 272E John Bragg inserted himself into the half-cirle of people at the Royal Entrance, having run from his traffic-directing post at the convergence of Bedford, Garrick and King Streets, Prince, with Graves in tow, had wandered a hundred yards east along Maiden Lane, almost as far as the Bedford Head pub, on the left-hand side. After getting the gist of what had happened, the constable went in pursuit. Graves, who must have been mightily relieved to see him, called out: 'I give this man in custody for stabbing.' As soon as Bragg had hold of Prince, Graves let him go. 'What's the matter?' Prince inquired. 'You know what,' Bragg replied, and straightway nudged him onwards, in the general direction of the Lyceum, the Theatres Royal of Drury Lane and Covent Garden, and, of peculiar significance, Bow Street Police Station.

It appears that Graves and Prince had not spoken to each other while they were, so to say, attached; but now they entered into conversation.

In reply to Graves's question, 'What could have induced you to do such a cruel deed as that?', Prince explained: 'Terriss would not employ me, and I was

determined to be revenged. He kept me out of work
for ten years.' When Graves hummed dubiously,
Prince snapped: 'I should have had either to die in the
streets or else have my revenge.'

At the police station, Constable Bragg handed his
prisoner over to Inspector George Wood; John Graves
made a brief statement and was then allowed to return
to the Adelphi. Perhaps because Bragg had been intent
on listening to and trying to remember Prince's
remarks, it had not occurred to him that Prince might
still be in possession of the knife he had used on
William Terriss. But that thought struck Inspector
Wood at once, and he ordered Prince to turn out his
pockets. As Prince produced the bloodstained knife, he
murmured to Bragg (whether or not jestingly, one
cannot tell): 'It is a good job for you that you didn't get
it.' Handing the knife to the inspector, he said: 'I gave
Terriss due warning, and if he is dead he knew what he
had to expect from me. He prevented me getting
assistance from the Actors' Benevolent Fund, and I
stabbed him.'

The only other items in his pockets were a pair of
black woollen gloves, so far beyond repair that they
looked as much like mittens, and a bundle of letters, all
from well-known people, most either acknowledging
the receipt of verses or expressing sympathy, or both;
of the rest, one was from the Duke and Duchess of
York, thanking Prince for his congratulations on the
birth of their son; one, on black-edged paper, was from
the Princess Henry of Battenberg, saying that she was
touched by his sentiments concerning her late husband,
and one was from William Gladstone, noting that he
was as pleased as was Prince that the River Dee was
now spanned by the Victoria Jubilee Bridge.

Since Inspector Wood was unsure of the gravity of
Prince's crime, he did not charge him before telling
Constable Bragg to take him to a cell. As Prince was
being led away, he burst into tears. The inspector asked

him what ailed him, expecting the answer to be contrition for his act or fear of the consequences. Prince said that he couldn't help crying, he was so hungry. He begged for food. Once he had been assured that he would be given some, he wiped his eyes on his sleeve and apologized for having made a scene.

At five minutes to eight – the time for the call of 'Act One, beginners' on any ordinary night – the silver key fell from William Terriss's hand, signifying his death. (Or so it is said. The trouble with stories that have a theatrical background is that the first tellers of them are apt to be lured into sacrificing exactness to dramatic unity: they speak of what should have happened as if it actually had. None of the three doctors who had hurried from the Charing Cross Hospital took a note, to the minute, of when, as a reporter would put it, 'the light of the star was extinguished for ever'.)

As has been mentioned, shortly after eight o'clock the assistant manager made an announcement from the stage; resultantly, the auditorium was soon empty save for its attendants.

By nine, special editions of newspapers, reporting Terriss's death, were being hawked in the West End. There was no special edition of the *Daily Telegraph*, but next morning that paper made news of the spreading of the news:

At first most people were incredulous, for tragedies of this kind are fortunately rare in the annals of our stage life, but when the fatal tidings were confirmed there was only one topic of discussion in the district occupied by the play-houses and throughout London, for the sad intelligence reached the clubs and other places where people foregather in an amazingly short time. All kinds of rumours – most of them contradictory, and some obviously absurd – were afloat as to the exact circumstances of the terrible crime, a fact which need excite no surprise when it is recollected that for some time after Mr Terriss had been attacked the greatest consternation prevailed in the theatre, and the immediate neighbourhood was in a state of ferment. A vast crowd of the curious and sympathetic flocked to the various entrances of the theatre, in the vain hope of learning details from the officials, and at one time the Strand was impassable. Neighbouring thoroughfares whence access may be had to the Adelphi were also filled by the multitude, whose faces, it was easy to see, expressed surprise and horror ....

Only the briefest interval elapsed before the dreadful news extended to the general public in the neighbourhood of the Strand. Of course, among the members of the profession it travelled apace, and general regrets and expressions of horror at the act were heard. The actors and actresses of the Adelphi company, as they came out of the theatre, passed away in twos and threes, talking in subdued tones of the distressing occurrence. It was evident that the remark of one actor to another as they came into the street: 'Good-night, old chap; I feel quite upset,' voiced the feelings of them all.

Mingling with the throng, one could easily see that, but for the corroboration given by the darkened theatre itself, the news would hardly have been credited. To the public Mr Terriss's figure was associated with deeds of bravery; so often had he portrayed before them the dashing, manly hero that there is no doubt that, as chance scraps of conversation showed, they saw him with the glamour of the stage upon him. To think of him, therefore, as dead by the cowardly hand of the assassin gave an intensified shock. 'Poor old Bill Terriss!' said a soldier in the crowd, 'if only he'd 'ad a chance, it wouldn't have been so bad. But it do seem a miserable death for 'im.'

At ten, Prince was roused from a sound sleep to be charged 'that he, about 7.20 p.m. on Thursday, the 16th of December, 1897, did kill and slay one William Terriss with a knife, in Maiden Lane in the Parish of St Margaret's'. He nodded and said, 'All right.' Asked if he had a relative or friend living in London whom he wished to be informed of his plight, he spoke of a married half-sister named Maggie. He said that he had chanced upon her only a few hours before, in the Strand, and had pleaded with her to give him ten shillings: 'If she had not refused me, this thing would never have happened.' A policeman was sent to her home. Upon his return, he told Prince that she wanted nothing to do with him. 'I didn't think she would,' Prince said. 'It is now clear that she was in league with Terriss.'

Shortly after midnight, Terriss's body, concealed in a basketwork shell, was carried from the Adelphi, through the main stage-door, and transported on a covered dray to the mortuary beneath the church of St Martin-in-the-Fields. There, an autopsy showed that the two stab-wounds in the back were severe, and might themselves have proved fatal, but that the wound in the breast was the cause of death. A cut on the left wrist indicated that Terriss had tried to deflect the frontal blow – which, the surgeon believed, had been struck with 'almost super-human force', for the weapon had pierced Terriss's coat, jacket, waistcoat and chest-protector, then almost severed the fifth rib, before penetrating the heart.

Throughout the night, the telephone and telegraph lines from Fleet Street were engrossed by questions, orders and requests, all in aid of adding to the bare details of the crime. As soon as it was known that Prince hailed from Dundee, 'stringers' of that city were alerted; and one of them, early from his bed, learned the address of Prince's mother, Margaret Archer, and called there.

Mrs Archer evidently knew nothing of the fearful event which had taken place in London, for she was anxious to learn the cause of so early a visit. 'Oh, it was about Dick?' and a happy smile played upon her features as she mentioned the name. 'He's in London, is Dick – an actor. Have I heard anything about him lately? Of course I have. My daughter had a letter from him only a day or two ago. Here it is,' and she drew the envelope from a rack near the fireplace.

The missive was written in a bold, clear hand – the letter of a man who could put a sentence together. But there seemed evidence of something being amiss with the writer. After a kindly query as to his mother's health, he relapsed into a desponding tone. He referred to the difficulty of getting work in London, and went on to say that he supposed there would be little use of him looking forward to visiting Dundee at Christmas. 'Just as well die in London' was the bitter observation with which he concluded.

Meanwhile, Mrs Archer had asked if anything was wrong with Dick, to which the only reply that could be given was that the young man had got into serious trouble in London. Intuitively, she seemed to conclude that to ask more would be to learn too much. However, she very courteous-ly, if at times huskily, continued to answer questions regarding her son.

Dick, as she called him, had always been a curious boy. When he was quite young he evinced a passion for the play, and night after night he spent within the walls of the old Theatre Royal in Castle Street. It was a happy night when he came home and confided to his parents that he had been taken on as a supernumerary at the theatre. This situation he kept for four years, working in a shipyard during the day and carrying out his stage duties in the evening. For the latter work he was paid at the rate of nine shillings a week, and that he was neither of a wild nor spendthrift disposition his mother testified. Richard's education had not been elaborate, but he was anxious to improve his mind, and with this in view he underwent a course of study, and gradually came to be regarded as a promising young fellow. The temporary removal of the household to London was the cause of Dick's throwing up his situation in Dundee, and he went to the metropolis a short time after his father and mother. 'He's a grand actor, our Dick,' said the old woman, and while under less depressing circumstances one could have admired the exhibition of maternal pride, it was terribly pathetic to listen to the mother's words of praise.

Previous to leaving Dundee on the last occasion, he had been idle for a considerable time, but he was hopeful of securing a post in some of the London theatres. The engagement which he looked for never came, however, hence the despairing nature of his last letter.

Replying to a question as to whether her son had ever spoken in a threatening manner of any person, Mrs Archer declared that she was not aware of his having the slightest animosity towards anyone in theatrical circles out of Dundee, although she remembered him once saying that he would like to do for one of the local officials. She never paid any attention to his threat.

'Now,' at last said Mrs Archer, 'I have told you all about Dick. Tell me what they have done to him. Is he locked up?' I answered that he was in the custody of the police. She covered her face with her hands and sobbed.

The public gallery of Bow Street Police Court was packed, in the main by actors and actresses, when, at half-past eleven on Friday morning, the door from the police station swung open and Richard Archer Prince made his entrance. No doubt he would have liked to pause, posing, in the doorway, but the two following constables marched inexorably, forcing him into the dock. The reception he got was uncertain at first, for hardly anyone in the audience knew him, not even by sight; however, the moment he entered the dock, there to stand pencil-straight, his Inverness buttoned to the throat and with the collar turned up, one hand holding his black slouch-hat, the fingers of the other preening his moustache, a chorus of boos, hisses and shouts of detestation filled the court. To his delight. He didn't mind being the villain; no, not at all. The important thing was that he was at last a star, standing centre-stage, playing to a full house. According to the reporter for the *Daily Telegraph*:

> During the hearing of the evidence the prisoner paid the closest possible attention to every detail, and watched the witnesses or Mr Wilson, who conducted the prosecution, with eyes that grew almost beadlike with the intensity of their concentration. Prince is said to be a Scotsman, but he possesses none of the outward characteristics of that race. On the contrary, his general appearance, his accent, and manner of speech are distinctly Italian, and the style in which the hair is worn in particular gives him a foreign look. One could not avoid the thought as one watched the man's movements in the dock that he was very self-conscious, and felt throughout that he was acting a part which must command the eyes and ears of his audience. It may have been entirely

unpremeditated on the part of the prisoner, but his every action appeared calculated for effect. He leant over the dock rail in a dramatic attitude for some time. When a statement was made by any of the witnesses to which he took exception, he shook his head slowly and smiled. No incident of the hearing disturbed his cool self-possession. At one point he turned round in the dock and took a comprehensive survey of the spectators, as if seeking for some familiar faces. Even the very dramatic moment when Inspector Wood slowly unfolded the fatal knife from its wrappings of paper and displayed it to the court had no effect upon him, though a perceptible shudder ran through everyone in court. A lethal weapon the knife looked. The blade had its bright steel reddened near the handle with an ominous stain.

In the prisoner's demeanour, after the cruel and terrible crime had been committed, as described by the witnesses, he showed no remorse for the deed or any desire to palliate or excuse it. Neither did he in court appear in the slightest to flinch from the consequences of it. He contradicted, in clear and unwavering tones, some of the statements of Mr Graves and Inspector Wood, and seemed to particularly resent the use of the word 'revenge' that was attributed to him. He denied that he had ever used that word, and said that 'blackmail' was the proper expression …. He was quick to profit by the warning from Sir John Bridge [the magistrate] not to make statements. He evinced no lack of nerve or courage.

At the close of the proceedings, when the magistrate decided to remand him, the prisoner exhibited the first symptom of concern, and complained that he had no solicitor. On being told that he might consult one before the next occasion when he would be brought before the

Court, he bowed to the magistrate, and walked from the dock unmoved by the unprecedented display of disgust and abhorrence of the foul crime which followed his retreating figure. Altogether the scene in court was a remarkable one. The intense eagerness of the spectators, and the sang-froid of the central figure, as the facts and circumstances of the crime were being narrated, formed a contrast not often seen in the courts, and one which must add, if possible, to the extraordinary feeling which has been excited by a dramatic crime.

In the nineteenth century, sensational murders often had commercial side-effects. The potters of Staffordshire turned out presentments of culprits and of the scenes of their crimes, printers rolled off catchpenny broadsheets, trial transcripts, and victim-commemorative cards that were suitable for framing (in February 1897, a London printer made, it might be said, a killing with unofficially-consecrated slices of pasteboard, Sacred to the Memory of Elizabeth Camp, a murdered barmaid, late of a pub called the Good Intent), and until the summer of 1868, when hangings in a good, legal cause were first carried out unpublicly, executioners and their reps made capital from the sale of cuttings of uniquely-used hemp – at half a crown per inch if the association was reckoned to justify that top rate – to sufferers from warts or the goitre or to people who were merely acquisitive of morbid mementoes. (Subsequent to public hangings – and to the public snipping of the respective means – the market was for a while glutted with chunks of hemp described as ex-executional; but then suspicion grew, demanding of the hawkers forgery of provenance prior to the spiel, and this additional chore caused most of them to revert to three-card trickery or to the offering of acceptedly-controversial splinters from the Cross.) Some murders

THE BLOOD STAINED KNIFE

MR. J. R. GRAVES, WHO WITNESSED THE MURDER.

187/1

Police Constable Bragg, 51 E.

THE MAGISTRATE EXAMINES THE FATAL KNIFE

SERGEANT BUSH.

PRISONER

PRISONERS ONLY

THE MURDERER LOUDLY HISSED ON LEAVING THE DOCK AT BOW STREET

TERRISS'S MURDERER IN COURT.
SKETCHES BY OUR SPECIAL ARTIST.

had a depressing effect on trade: in 1871, a national partiality to chocolate creams was diminished by the news that Miss Christiana Edmunds, who could hardly have been more genteel, had injected several of such confections with strychnine, her object being to bereave the doctor she adored of his sweet-toothed wife, leaving the coast of Brighton clear for her own pursuance of matrimony; and, if one believes the legend, Mrs Marie Manning's choice of material for her going-away gown, remarked upon by thousands, Charles Dickens among them, who craned their necks as she was hanged on the roof of Horsemonger Lane Gaol in 1849 for the murder of a one-time beau, had an adverse effect on the fashionableness of black satin.

So far as I can tell, there is no footnote to the annals of crime, no aside from a stage-person's memoirs, no parenthesis in a history of the retailing of textiles, observing that on Friday, 17 December 1897, the haberdashers of the West End and its environs experienced a rush for slight offcuts of black crepe that all but the oldest of them, at least forty-five years in the business and so theoretically capable of recalling a similar rush following the demise of the Iron Duke, thought unprecedented; or that, during the remaining fortnight of the year, any man noticeable in the street in any event but made more so by his wearing of an armband of mourning was, ten to one, a member of the theatrical profession. Each phenomenon, the first contributing to the second, certainly occurred. Of course, much as some people today wear sweatshirts publicizing causes that they do not support, some of the ostensible mourners of William Terriss felt no pang at his passing but had black tacked to their sleeves because they liked the idea of being labelled, albeit temporarily, as thespians.

But, no doubt of it, the counterfeit mourners were vastily outnumbered by the genuine. Headlines such as A PROFESSION GRIEVES told a truth. The stage weekly,

The Era, spoke for as well as to its readers in the issue hastened from the press for sale on the Friday night:

> The excitement, the agitation, have subsided; and all that remains is a deep, benumbing sorrow .... In all circles of society, from the mansions of the West End to the slums of the East, there are faithful friends and honest admirers mourning for the dead actor and execrating his cowardly assassin. The first feeling must have been one of awe, for it is an awesome thought that this actor, young at least in virile energy, manly spirit, and the enjoyment of life, should have been cut down in the full bloom and flower of his popularity and prosperity. We can hardly realize, even yet, that Terriss – the hearty, honest, buoyant, breezy Terriss – lies a mere mass of still, cold clay; that the mobile features are fixed and waxen, the eloquent eyes are glazed and stony, and the strong, active body is stiffened into a spiritless corpse. And when it comes home to us as a cruel, wretched reality, the truth is too terrible and the bitterness is greater than we can bear.

The Adelphi was dark (and would remain so until the morning of Boxing Day, when *Secret Service* would be revived, with Herbert Waring playing Terriss's part, and May Whitty[1] replacing Jessie Millward, still

---

1. Now best remembered as the Lady who Vanished in the film that Alfred Hitchcock made in 1938 of Ethel Lina White's novel *The Wheel Spins*. In 1918, she became the first actress to be created a Dame Commander of the Order of the British Empire – though for services in connection with the Great War rather than for her stage work; the American-born Genevieve Ward was the first actress to be honoured as such, by being made a Dame in 1921; four years later, Ellen Terry, who most people considered should have been the first actress-Dame (the general suspicion was that she was passed over on acount of her having been thrice married), became the second.

inconsolable, as Miss Varney); but that is not to say
that the theatre was a forsaken place.

From early on Friday, Henry Spratt, custodian at the
stage-door, hardly had a minute to himself, was rarely
upright between bows, as one important person after
another entered, dishevelled from contact with the
crowds of reporters and spectators at one end or the
other of Bull Inn Court, which was kept clear by
cordoning constables, to express sorrow to the Gatti
brothers and, through them, to the Terriss family.
Most of the visitors were connected with the stage
(these included the three actor-knights, Henry Irving,
Squire Bancroft and Charles Wyndham) but some were
hereditarily noble, and at least one (Sir Henry Haw-
kins, who refused to tether his terrier outside, snapping
magisterially that 'Jack' accompanied him in all un-
ecclesiastic places) was a member of the Queen's
Bench.

Hundreds of telegrams, thousands of letters and
cards, were delivered to the Adelphi; on some, the
address was scanty or inventive, or both – to 'Terriss's
Playhouse, London', for instance – and nearly all were
meant to be read by Terriss's widow. The latter fact
turned out to contain a complication. Early on, the
clerk assigned by Arthur Latham, the manager of the
theatre, to sort the missives into piles, the eventually
largest of these to be tidied away into sacks and
transported by hansom to The Cottage at Turnham
Green, noticed that the writer of one card, oblivious of
Amy Terriss, had assumed that the widow was Jessie
Millward: a pardonable error considering that
husband-and-maiden-named-wife stage-partnerships
were common and that during the last few years of
William Terriss's celebrity, Amy had become almost
reclusive, rarely venturing from the house, not even to
attend her husband's first nights, and never, but never,
aiding the concoctors of Green-Room Gossip columns
(who, quite likely, relished her reticence, which allo-

wed them to be venturesome with innuendo about an offstage – or rather, behind-the-scenes – relationship between the male and female stars of the Adelphi).

Apprised of the card-writer's misapprehension, Arthur Latham ordered the clerk to add censorship to the sorting task; to winkle away from the Turnham Green-intended pile any condolences to the widow that might distress her by their faulty guesswork as to who she was. As it turned out, the carefulness was unnecessary: after one consignment of mail had been delivered to The Cottage, Amy wrote to Arthur Latham, thanking him all the same, but saying that she could not bring herself to read any of the countless messages she was receiving direct, let alone forwarded ones; a day or so later, her son Tom (Ellaline's younger brother; himself a stage performer, though without distinguishment) spoke on her behalf to the press, explaining 'the impossibility of replying individually to the great number of manifestations of affection and sympathy, and trusting that a general acknowledgment would suffice'. It seems probable that Amy made an exception to her non-reading, non-replying decisions – that being in the case of a message from Queen Victoria, the Widow of Windsor, who asserted that Her sorrow was shared by all Her subjects, in Great Britain and far-flung throughout the world: an extent of emotion that, what with the suffusion of Empire Pink on the globe, left relatively few people untouched.

Within a short while of Terriss's death, the Adelphi management had telegraphed the news to William Gillette, who was in Pittsburgh, heading a *Secret Service* road company. Gillette's immediate, wired response augmented, and confirmed a part of, the Queen's generalization:

UNSPEAKABLY SHOCKED. WE MOURN DEATH OF TERRISS WITH ALL WHO LOVED HIM, WHICH MEANS ALL ENGLAND.

The press-requested comments of Terriss's native fellows tended to be quietly recollective: more in keeping with the new 'natural' style of drama, leaving the audience to worry for meanings between the lines, than with the declamatory sort. But George Alexander, the actor-manager who had made himself as much at home at the St James's as had Terriss at the Adelphi (though, two years before, he had been forced to cut short the inaugural run of *The Importance of Being Earnest* owing to the tribulations and trials of the play's author – who had once complained of him that he did not act on the stage: he behaved), came up with a speech that would have satisfied any of the Adelphi melodramatists:

> Will Terriss was a man to the finger-tips. Nature stood up and said it to all the world; and by his death the modern stage loses some of its virile force.
> Lie lightly on him, Earth.

George Edwardes, of the Gaiety, recalled Terriss as

> one of the most generous men I knew. About two months ago, he was in my office when an application was brought to me for help from a poor actor. I showed it to him. 'Well,' he remarked with a smile, 'if you give to every one in this way, you will finish up in the workhouse.' Afterwards I had a conversation with the applicant, who admitted that only a week before, Terriss had sent him £10.

The vocalist and actress Florence St John exclaimed, 'Poor old Willie!' and went on:

> The last time I saw him was when he called on me on the night of last Saturday week, after the production of *The Grand Duchess*.[1] I was feeling

1. The English libretto of this comic opera, with music by

a bit depressed, but he cheered me up with these words, which I little dreamed would be the last I should ever hear from him: 'Never mind, Jack; so long as you have a few pals and your health, you're all right.'[1]

Henry Irving's business-manager Bram Stoker, whose tale of vampirism, *Dracula*, had been published earlier in the year, thought back to 1883,

when the Lyceum company were crossing to America on the *City of Rome*. A rather bragging man, seeing so many landmen present, not like himself in yachting rig, pulled out a ten-pound note, and openly offered to bet that not one of the passengers would take his cap off the top of the mast. Terriss instantly covered the note, and, throwing off his coat, tightened his belt. 'Done,' he said; 'up with you and put it on. I will follow and take it off.' The offer was withdrawn.

Offenbach, was written by Charles Brookfield, who, in 1895, when he was playing the small part of Phipps, the butler, in the first production of *An Ideal Husband*, moonlighted industriously as a seeker of evidence in support of the Marquess of Queensberry's assertion that the play's author, Oscar Wilde, was 'Posing as Somdomite' [sic].

1.   Terriss's words indicate that he was unaware that a probable reason why Miss St John was 'feeling a bit depressed' was that an actor named Francis Carroll, who was as unsuccessful as Prince, was threatening to murder her. In the following February, Carroll – of Buckingham Road, Brighton – was convicted of having sent threatening letters to her and to his father, a retired army officer. In default of finding sureties in the sum of £100 for his good behaviour for one year, he was given a prison sentence of six months. His first action when he was returned to his cell was to pick up a plate of food intended as his dinner and hurl it at the gaoler. However, subsequent disciplining seems to have mellowed him: I can find no indication that, following his release, he used the Royal Mail objectionably.

During the week in which Terriss was murdered, the Lyceum company was at the Grand Theatre, Wolverhampton. Of course, Stoker was not the only person associated with the company to be asked for a quote. The entry for 16 December in Ellen Terry's diary records:

> Willie Terriss was murdered this evening Newspapers sent me a wire for 'expressions of sympathy'!!

As will appear, her shock at the news may have been accompanied by a worry concerning a practical effect of Terriss's death on a friend. For the present, all she would tell the reporters was that she could not tell them anything:

> The whole affair is so terrible, and I feel it so deeply, as all who knew him must, that I really cannot talk of it.

Irving – called 'guv'nor' by Terriss, even when he was no longer a Lyceumite – was more forthcoming:

> Some of us have his words – confident, cheery words – still ringing in our ears. Only two days ago he was with me, arranging for the production of *The Corsican Brothers* at the Adelphi – a play with which he had intimate associations in his Lyceum days – and it is strange that, with that grim drama in his mind, he should have been struck down by a murderous hand.

One of Terriss's friends at the Green Room Club must have been surprised, perhaps saddened, to learn that he had planned yet another revival of *The Corsican Brothers*. Three weeks before, just after the opening of *Secret Service*, Terriss had confided in the man: 'I'm longing to appear in a new style of drama. I'm tired of being accused of murder every night, and being proved innocent about eleven o'clock.'

It seems that that last comment was spoken tongue-in-cheek, because Terriss was thinking of surprising the theatrical world, not once but twice: first with the announcement that he was to star in a new play by the foremost new-style dramatist, Bernard Shaw, who as a drama critic had lambasted Irving at the Lyceum, Terriss at the Adelphi, for squandering their talents on tosh – and then with the play itself, which would mock those melodramas, staple of the Adelphi, in which the hero made a series of mighty bounds between predicaments, at last coming to rest, clutching the girl of his dreams, and with sufficient breath left to utter a speech on some worthy topic, just before the curtain fell.

Ellen Terry was one of the few people who knew of Terriss's intention; of Shaw's play, which was called *The Devil's Disciple*. Not until more than thirty years later – in 1931, when the correspondence between Shaw and Ellen Terry, by then dead, was published – was it possible to piece together an account of the making of the play that, but for Richard Archer Prince's intervention, William Terriss might have presented in London, not only starring as Dick Dudgeon, a copy of his stage-self, but also amending the script here and there, perhaps saliently in some of the scenes. Though futile, it is fascinating to wonder how different the play would be from its published form if the actor who bespoke it had lived to trim it, Shaw approving and assisting, towards a perfect fit.

The first Ellen Terry heard of the project was from a letter that Shaw (whom she had never met) wrote to her on 26 March 1896:

> ... Terriss (this is a secret) wants me to collaborate with him in a play, the scenario of which includes every situation in the Lyceum repertory or the Adelphi record. The best act is The Bells.[1] He is

1. Irving's first season at the Lyceum, in 1871, was unsuccessful till his appearance as Mathias, the unapprehended murderer

arrested either for forgery or murder at every curtain, and goes on as fresh as paint and free as air when it goes up again. I talked it over with him whilst he was dressing for a matinée at the Adelphi. I noticed that his chest was black and blue. He caught the expression of pity and horror in my eyes as I caught sight of the bruise, and said, with a melancholy smile, 'Ah yes, Ellen Terry! You remember the third act of Olivia at the old Court? I was Thornhill. The marks have never come off. I shall carry them to my grave.'[1] I did not tell him that I also had received heart wounds in those days which I shall carry to my grave. Neither, by the way, did I decide in favour of the collaboration. But I seriously think I shall write a play for him. A good melodrama is a more

who suffers from ringing in the ears, in *The Bells*, adapted by Leopold Lewis, a solicitor, from *Le Juif Polonais* by M. M. Erckmann-Chatrian.

When Lewis died, in February 1890, the editor of *The Stage* wrote: 'Poor fellow, at one time it was said of him that *The Bells* had made him, as he was wont to boast that the same play had made Irving. As a matter of fact, I think *The Bells* ruined him. His success was too much for him, and ever since its production he has been steadily going down the hill. One of his most faithful friends was Mr Irving, and it is from the Lyceum manager that Mr Lewis received many little acts of thoughtful kindness of which the world will, I suppose, for ever remain in ignorance.'

1. If Shaw's anecdote is true, then Terriss had already carried the marks for nearly eighteen years, an extraordinary time for bruises to remain visible. Admittedly, accounts of the Court production of *Olivia* indicate that Ellen Terry did not pull her punches. One cannot say whether Shaw was more or less impressed by the breast-beating 'business', witnessed by him from the stalls in 1878, than by the lingering effects of it on Terriss's person; but, either way, he borrowed the business for a stage direction in *You Never Can Tell*, which he appears to have completed in June 1896.

difficult thing to write than all this clever-clever comedy: one must go straight to the core of humanity to get it, and if it is only good enough, there you have Lear or Macbeth ....

Shaw to Ellen Terry, 30 November 1896:

... I finished my play today. What do you think of that? Does that look like wasting my time? Three acts, six scenes, a masterpiece, all completed in a few weeks, with a trip to Paris and those Ibsen articles thrown in – articles which were so over-written that I cut out and threw away columns. Not to mention the Bradford election ....

What did I want so particularly to say? Oh yes, it was this. I have written to Terriss to tell him that I have kept my promise to him and have 'a strong drama' with a part for him; but I want your opinion; for I have never tried melodrama before, and this thing, with its heroic sacrifice, its impossible court martial, its execution (imagine W.T. *hanged* before the eyes of the Adelphi!), its sobbings and speeches and declamations, may possibly be the most farcical absurdity that ever made an audience shriek with laughter. And yet I have honestly tried for dramatic effect. I think you could give me a really *dry* opinion on it; for it will not tickle you, like Arms and the Man and You Never Can Tell, not get at your sympathetic side like Candida (the heroine is not the hero of the piece this time); and you will have to drudge conscientiously through it like a stage carpenter and tell me whether it is a burlesque or not.

But now that I think of it, all this is premature. The play only exists as a tiny scrawl in my note books – things I carry about in my pockets. I shall have to revise it and work out all the stage business, besides reading up the history of the

American War of Independence before I can send it to the typist to be readably copied. Meanwhile I can read it to Terriss, and to other people, but not to – well, no matter: I dont ask that the veil of the temple shall be rent: on the contrary, I am afraid, in my very soul, to come stumping in my thickbooted, coarse, discordant reality, into that realm where a magic Shaw, a phantasm, a thing who looks delicate and a boy (twelve stalls and a bittock off) poses fantastically before a really lovely Ellen ....

Now I have finished my play, nothing remains but to kiss my Ellen once and die.

The reading of the play to Terriss did not go as Shaw would have wished, he told an *Observer* journalist in 1930: Terriss heard little of it as he could not keep awake. However, Ellen Terry drudged remarkably conscientiously through the copy of the script that Shaw had sent to her. On 7 March 1897, she wrote:

Yes, the 2nd Act was so tremendous, it 'took it out of me' as they say. So I tried to *wait* for Act III and lay flat on the diningroom table for a while! Fidgeted, then got up and went at it again. 'You'll rewrite it?' Oh now *do* like a pet. No softening. No, no. Nothing of that kind. 'Tell you how'?!! Why you have been working on it for months! How could I tell you 'how' all in a minute, and with Sans-Gêne, and headaches and things. I'll get someone to read it to me over and over again, and then I'll tell you what I think. And if a lot of my 'thinks' could be of a wee bit of use to you should not I be a proud lady! It struck me at once that those scenes between Burgoyne and Swindon (although they are excellent scenes *as scenes* and *for acting*) are irritating as interruptions, like Lovers talking of Ships or Icebergs that pass in the night when they dont feel quite like that. Then too 3 scenes in one act (and that the *last act*) is clumsy (Oh, excuse me! Ignorant and rude!), unfortunate. I think I've turned the corner and am getting better. But this ghastly weather is frustrating. Cant write. Oh, that 2nd Act! There has never been anything in the least like it. You *are* a Dear ....

People are so odd that I'm certain no one could compete with T. as Dick. The neat head and figure, and the charm, the arrogant manner. 'Taking.' Act II will find out the *woman* ....

Another copy of the script had been sent, or would soon be sent, to the American actor-manager Richard Mansfield, who had produced and starred in two of Shaw's plays, *Arms and the Man* and *Candida*, in that country. In Shaw's letter of 26 March 1896 to Ellen Terry, letting her into the secret of what had passed between himself and Terriss in the star's dressing-room, he had referred to his short play *The Man of Destiny* (in which the character of the Strange Lady was modelled on Ellen Terry), saying that he was thinking of allowing it to 'be done ... in America by Mansfield, who has had the audacity to ask me for another play, after heaping villainy on me over my Candida'. And Ellen Terry had added a postscript to her letter of 3 September 1896: 'One word about the little play (and breathe it to a living creature, and ugh! what is there I wont do to you?). If you let the little man [Mansfield] play it, it will be of little count, for he's rather clever, but not enough clever. In the first place he'd play it as it is, uncut, and Lord help you both then! For, although I love every word of it, it is too long in certain places to *play-act* as it now stands. All well, as it stands, to read, but not to play-act.' Mansfield presented *The Devil's Disciple* (presumably, as it was), he himself as Dick Dudgeon, at Albany on 1 October 1897, and the following week at the Fifth

Avenue Theatre, New York; despite poor reviews, the production became Shaw's first great box-office success, enabling him to give up regular journalism so as to concentrate on the writing of plays.

But as for a London production, Shaw told Ellen Terry on 24 December 1897:

> My calculations are quite put out by the unforeseen extinction of Terriss. I was scheming to get the D.'s D. produced with him in the part and Jessie Millward as Judith. The alternative was a [Herbert] Waring and [Arthur] Bourchier combination – Bourchier to play Burgoyne. And now Terriss is only a name and a batch of lies in the newspapers, and Waring goes to the Adelphi in his place. However, Waring may need stronger plays than Terriss, who was a play in himself; so perhaps Jessie may play Judith yet ....

In her reply, written two days later, Ellen Terry remarked that 'the D.D. would be best now I think with [Charles] Wyndham who would I should say revel in the part', and went on:

> Poor Willie Terriss, I'll miss him. That calling him 'Breezy Bill' always annoyed me. So vulgar and so very stupid to call him that. Poor Jessie M.!

Shaw, unable to believe his eyes when he saw the suggestion that Wyndham should play Dick Dudgeon, wrote back at once: 'It would be impossible: he's too old; and he has not the peculiar fascination.' After allowing that the sixty-year-old Wyndham 'would be admirable as the husband: it would suit him to a hair's breadth', and musing on other casting possibilities, Shaw concluded:

> I should like to get the piece on at the Adelphi with Waring in order to secure Jessie's part for her.

What actually happened was not at all to Shaw's liking. *The Devil's Disciple* was not presented in England until 26 September 1899 – and then tattily, without benefit of stars, at the Princess of Wales's Theatre in that drab part of London called Kennington, where it lasted only a fortnight. Eight more years elapsed before it was seen in the West End, as a component of Harley Granville-Barker's repertory season, retrospectively reckoned epoch-making for presentational style, at the Savoy, across the Strand from the Adelphi; Matheson Lang played the part of Dick Dudgeon – of William Terriss.

Richard Archer Prince: he, too, had written a play. *Countess Otto*, it was called. Penned in pale-violet ink in penny exercise-books, these sewn together at their top left-hand corners, the script had grown dog-eared from many submissions by the autumn of 1896, when Prince, saving on postage so as to afford his fare home to Dundee, delivered it, in a broken envelope marked 'For the Kind Attention of Mr Fred Terry', at the stage-door of the Royalty Theatre in Dean Street, off Shaftesbury Avenue. Weeks passed; and then Prince, having received only an acknowledgment from Fred Terry, began to inundate the actor with correspondence, on some days – damn the expense to his mother – posting three or four letters or cards. Terry returned the script; but, trying to soften the accompanying note of rejection, said that the play had no parts suitable for himself or for his wife Julia Neilson – a comment that Prince twisted into meaning that Terry had been henpecked into turning down *Countess Otto*. The next thing was that Julia Neilson – playing Princess Flavia in *The Prisoner of Zenda* at the St James's – started receiving missives from Dundee. However, by Christmas, Prince had run out of steam – or his mother of stamps – and Fred and Julia Terry were forgetting their pesterer.

But months later, and then for weeks to come, Fred Terry was made aware that Prince was back in town. Terry, you see, often chaired meetings of the emergency committee of the Actors' Benevolent Fund. He was the 'one of the Terrys' mentioned to Prince, the denied applicant, on Wednesday, 15 December 1897.

The following night, he, like his sister Ellen, heard from reporters what had happened by the Adelphi, and was asked for an 'expression of sympathy'. Off the cuff, he supplied: 'Will Terriss has left us, mourned by many, regretted by all.' He was now working with his wife at the St James's. After the performance, while driving to their home on Primrose Hill, they spoke more of Prince than of Terriss; and next morning they rummaged through box-files of old letters in search of evidences of the long-running *Countess Otto* correspondence. All that remained were a couple of cards, both postmarked '9.30 p.m., 23 Nov 96', and an undated letter.

One of the cards read:

> 68 Hill Street, Dundee
> Sir – Please return Play 'Countess Otto' at once. If you are hard up for money will send it. Terriss, the Pope and Scotland Yard, I will answer in a week. – RICHARD A. PRINCE

The message on the other card, presumably written following receipt of the script, contained another mysterious allusion:

> 68 Hill Street, Dundee
> Sir – Favour to hand this morning at ten o'clock. The old story about King Charles and the two hundred thousand pounds. They sold him for a King. I'm only a Prince. But a woman, mon Dieu, a woman. – RICHARD A. PRINCE

The letter read:

51 William Street, Vic Road, Dundee
Late Union Jack Tours
To Mrs Fred Terry
Madam – I thank you as a 'Highlander and a
gentleman,' and in the name of the Almighty
God, our Queen, and my rights for play 'Coun-
tess of Otto'. I am, Madam, yours faithfully,

RICHARD A. PRINCE

On the reverse of the sheet was a wonderfully
irrelevant postscript, something to do with the troubles
besetting the 'Godly' King of Greece.

Though it must have struck Fred Terry that the
dropping of Terriss's name, among those of more
illustrious others, would intrigue the police, he chose
to show the communications to a journalist on the
Daily Telegraph, thus enabling that paper – as carefree
with comment on cases that were *sub judice* as were its
rivals – to speak most authoritatively about Prince: 'a
monomaniac who has gradually developed the homicidal tendency.'

Following Fred Terry's lead, less-renowned members of his profession who had had dealings with
Prince decided to help the press, rather than the police,
with their enquiries. For instance, Ralph Croyden,
manager of Miss Lena Develrey's London Theatrical
Company – 'presently delighting audiences at the
Princess Theatre, Leith' – spoke 'exclusively' to several
special correspondents about his encounters with
Prince, the first on the evening of Saturday, 23 October
1897, at the Amphitheatre, Newcastle-upon-Tyne.
(One cannot be sure, but it seems that Prince, having
heard or read of a vacancy in Miss Develrey's company, was so desperate for work that he had travelled
all the way to Newcastle on the offchance of getting the
job.) Mr Croyden recalled that

Prince detailed his experiences as an actor, and
explained that he had played important parts at

the Adelphi, London, most especially in *The Union Jack*. He had, he said, been wronged – deadly wronged – by one of the leading lights of the stage, and there was only one man in the world whom he hated, and he was Mr Terriss. In reply to a question why he left the Adelphi, Prince said that it was because Mr Terriss was a man whom he could not stand. Mr Terriss had got on purely through influence, while he, a poor dog, had to work his way up. Although suspicious of Prince on account of certain peculiarities which he presented, I engaged him.

It had been arranged that the company were to appear at the theatre in Hetton-le-Hole, twelve or fourteen miles out of Newcastle, on Monday evening, the pieces to be played being *Nurse Charity* and *Parson Thorne*, and the parts – they were minor parts – assigned to Prince being Sir Leycester Lightfoot in the former and Sir Geoffrey Dashwood in the latter. Prince received copies of his parts for the purpose of studying them, and before he left I invited him to tea on the Sunday afternoon. My wife belongs to Scotland, and when Prince arrived I told her that a Scotsman had come to see her. She expressed delight, whereupon Prince, assuming a melodramatic attitude and waving his right arm, exclaimed, to the surprise of everyone present, 'My name's Mac-Gregor, and I'll smoke a clay-pipe if I like.' He had, he subsequently explained, been with another theatrical company, and had been discharged because he smoked a clay-pipe instead of a cigar. He scarcely ever ceased speaking of and vowing vengeance on Mr Terriss, and the party came to the conclusion that he was mentally deranged.

We had reserved five compartments of the train that was to take us from Newcastle to

Hetton. Prince duly turned up and joined the party at the station, but he declined to travel with any of us and occupied a compartment to himself. On reaching our destination, we at once proceeded to the theatre for a rehearsal. Then it appeared that Prince was utterly incompetent to speak anything. He, in turn, tugged at the hair of his head, rolled his eyes in a wild fashion, and pressed his temples.

In the circumstances, I found myself in a rather awkward predicament. At length, I told Prince that he had better go away. On this, Prince raved over his experiences at the Adelphi, declared what a fine actor he was, and pleaded that the performance might be postponed till the following evening. This, of course, was out of the question, and eventually I and some associates got rid for the time being of our disagreeable companion.

Next morning, Prince was early astir. He called at the house where my wife and I were staying no less than five times before I found it convenient to see him. When admitted into the room, he demanded some money. The fact of the matter was, he said, that his head went wrong at times, and he could not think what he was doing, thinking of his vengeance. Naturally enough, I declined to give him any money. Thereupon he became more excited than before, and used threatening language. He remarked that he was 'not strong enough to fight with you now, but tomorrow I will come and have my vengeance'. I ordered him out of the house as a madman, and he retaliated by raising his walking-stick, and saying:

'Mad, mad, mad! You will hear of my madness. The world will ring with it.'

By the time twilight fell on Monday, 20 December, the eve of the funeral, the conservatory of The Cottage was unseasonally floral, crammed with tributes in many forms and from all sorts of people.[1] Nosegays from

---

1. Financial contributions towards a Terriss Memorial were pouring in to the organizer's office at the *Daily Telegraph:* £1,126 in all (roughly the equivalent of 35,000 present-day pounds).

From *Just a Little Bit of String* by Ellaline Terriss (London 1955): 'There was no thought of a statue or something which would do little or no good. Instead of that, to the memory of the man who had loved the sea, and sailed it, who had saved life from its clutch, who had been a hero of *Harbour Lights*, they erected a lifeboat house at Eastbourne, bearing his name. And from that house his lifeboat saved many lives. My father would have been overjoyed at that.'

From the *Eastbourne Local History Society Newsletter*, No. 26 (circa 1975): 'The foundation stone of the William Terriss Lifeboat House was laid by the Duchess of Devonshire (also at that time Mayoress of Eastbourne) on 16 July 1898 .... The new lifeboat house was to be built at the foot of the eastern slopes of the Wish Tower Hill, and a marquee was erected over the spot where the foundation stone was to be laid. Gaily decked with bunting, the lifeboat, with the crew aboard, was drawn by horses from the old boathouse at the rear of the Wish Tower grounds. The band of the Sussex Artillery Militia played and the Eastbourne Cadet Corps formed a guard of honour. After the Duchess arrived in her carriage, the ceremonies began. Many letters and telegrams were read from friends and associates of William Terriss .... After a brief religious service, the Duchess tapped the stone with a mallet and declared the stone well and truly laid.

'Until 1924 the William Terriss Memorial Lifeboat House housed an active boat. For thirteen years after that, it only held a boat for demonstration purposes. On 22 March 1937 it was opened as a lifeboat museum, the first of its kind in the country. It was opened by Sir Godfrey Baring, Chairman of the Royal National Lifeboat Institution. Ellaline Terriss attended and made a short speech.'

From *The Lifeboat*, June 1937: 'A tablet on a wall of the William Terriss Memorial Lifeboat House records that it is "From those who loved and admired him" .... On one of the

Terriss's humble friends, admirers and servants drooped in the crevices between ingenious creations ordered by those who could afford to express themselves extravagantly: ladders, globes, masks of Tragedy, lyres (one from Dan Leno), haloes (one from the Prince of Wales), hearts, prosceniums, and books (or were they playscripts?), both open and closed. Not all of the tributes were waiting there; some had gone straight to Brompton Cemetery – among these, Jessie Millward's, which was a cushion of white chrysanthemums with the words 'To My Dear Comrade' spelt out in purple anemones.

Ellen Terry kept company with Jessie that night. She afterwards wrote to Shaw: 'Poor little Jessie … seemed so wee and crumpled up. I hope she will get good work. She will need help now.'[1]

The cortège set off on its five-mile journey, timed by Terriss's stage-manager to take an hour, at noon. Right at the start, something happened that one of the dozens of reporters scribbled down as 'an incident unrehearsed by Man that yet seemed too perfectly theatrical to be ascribed to coincidence'. As the head of the cortège was passing beneath the railway bridge by Turnham Green Station, a train was passing, just as slowly, overhead. 'It was filled with soldiers, and the redcoats, bent upon adding their tribute to the rest, gave three lusty cheers

walls is a portrait of William Terriss, presented to the museum by his daughter.'

The museum still exists.

1. Reporting her death, at the age of 71, in July 1932, *The Times* noted that, 'after the murder, it needed a great force to compel or cajole Miss Millward to enter a theatre again. That force was at hand in [the American impresario] Charles Frohman. In 1898 he persuaded her to go to the United States of America, and there she stayed till 1913, with only one short break in 1906. After her return, she played a little in suburban theatres and on tour.'

for the actor upon whose words and deeds they had so often hung.'

The *Daily Mail:*

Few could have anticipated the remarkable demonstration of interest and respect which imparted to the funeral the dignity of a public ceremonial. Throughout the route to the cemetery the streets were lined with people who silently watched the procession pass, while in the cemetery it is computed that the sorrowing assembly numbered many thousands.

Long before the cemetery was reached dense crowds lined and blocked the streets. And the multitude which thronged the avenues and was dispersed over the vast burial ground was

AN ORDERLY MASS,

patient and silent in the eager east wind; not deeply moved, perhaps. Indeed, it would be misleading to assert that any such wave of emotion was perceptible as often sways a multitude when one of its idols goes untimely to his death.

But its deep respect was shown in many striking ways. There was a kindliness abroad. Not even the biting cold and the long hours of weary waiting could affect that. The people were mostly drawn from the lowlier ranks to whom the dead actor's art specially appealed. They had come to be present at the final scene, to see his last part played in deathly silence.

And when the open hearse drawn by four horses had passed, and the long string of mourning coaches and carriages had filed slowly by, many thousands quietly re-covered their bared heads and sadly wended their way home.

Around the oak coffin, as it stood within the chapel, upon a catafalque draped with purple velvet, as around the open grave, well-known faces were to be seen on every side. Actors, managers, singers, playwrights – the London stage had sent all the most famous of its favourites to discharge the last debt of comradeship to their dear friend. They went

FOR THE MOST PART UNRECOGNIZED

by the huge concourse which gazed across the large roped-in enclosure around the grave, but many eyes were centred on the tall, stately figure of Sir Heny Irving escorting Miss Millward, both stricken with grief.

Some people had dreaded, and others had looked forward to, a confrontation between Terriss's widow and his 'dear comrade'; but this did not take place, because Amy was not among the visible mourners. Though, of course, her absence gave rise to unkind rumours, it is probable that she was either too ill to attend or ordered not to by a doctor: eight months later, she died from cancer. One gathers that Shaw, himself an absentee, read an account of the funeral but was too taken by the vignette of Irving and Jessie to observe the omission of Amy's name from the columns-long list of mourners. He wrote to Ellen Terry:

H.I. scored nobly by standing by [Jessie] at the funeral: had it been his funeral, Lady Irving would have been in the position of Mrs Terriss; and you would have been – probably taking a nice drive through Richmond Park with me, or perhaps with that villain you persuaded me you were going to marry the other day. Jessie must have been consoled a little; for she adores H.I. and always reserved his claims, as an intellectual prince, before Terriss's, greatly to William's indignation; for he knew that Henry was intellectually an imposter, nothing like so hardheaded as himself.

I have said that one of the lyre-wreaths was from Dan Leno. Another was from Ellaline Terriss; the attached card read, 'To darling old father, from his devoted, heart-broken daughter, Ellie.' Directly after the murder, Seymour Hicks had considered keeping it secret from her for the time being, fearing that the shock might cause a relapse; still undecided when he next went to the hospital, he was left with no alternative but to tell her by the sight of a pack of reporters roaming near her ward.

The last card to her father was written from the hospital, but shortly afterwards she was deemed well enough to leave. By the following August, when her mother died, she was touring as the Girl in a Gaiety musical. Her share of the estate amounted to a substantial sum (William Terriss's will was proved at £18,809, the equivalent, roughly speaking, of half a million present-day pounds), and this, added to over the next few years from her increasingly high earnings as a stage-performer, and from those of her husband as both playwright and actor, enabled Hicks to team up with Charles Frohman to build two theatres in the West End: first, the Aldwych, near the Gaiety and intended to be its competitor as a musical-comedy house, which opened in December 1905 with a revival of *Bluebell in Fairyland*, Hicks's 'musical dream-play', starring himself and Ellaline (and with a girl called Gladys Cooper, just seventeen, playing a small role), and second, the Hicks, in Shaftesbury Avenue, which opened almost exactly a year later, the first production being *The Beauty of Bath*, partly written by Hicks and with his wife starring, which was transferred from the Aldwych; in 1909, the Hicks was rechristened the Globe, the name under which the theatre still flourishes.

The husband-and-wife stage-partnership lasted for half a century, till 1949, when Hicks died; he had been knighted fourteen years before, and then it had been said that the honour was actually a joint tribute, earned equally by 'Lady Ellie'. As if making up for the curtailment of her parents' lives, she lived to be a hundred, qualifying for a congratulatory telegram from the Queen. Upon her death in June 1971, obituarists mentioned that she was the daughter of an actor known as William Terriss, and felt the need to explain that he too had been a star.

The last act of what most of the papers entitled The Adelphi Tragedy was played out at the Theatre Royal, Old Bailey – correctly called the Central Criminal Court – on Thursday, 13 January 1898. No; that date, four weeks from that of the commission of the crime, is not a misprint. Nor is there error in the indication that the proceedings were completed within a day. If you are surprised or, being liberal, shocked by such speeds, then you have been taken in by the legal profession, which has, only since the 1950s, made an ersatz virtue of both dilatoriness in the preparation of criminal cases for trial and elongation of the proceedings, thereby profiting many of its members at the expense of, inter alia, Justice.

Following the try-out at Bow Street, Richard Archer Prince had been lodged with other prisoners on custodial remand, in the hospital wing of Holloway Gaol. There, he had eaten, if not well, with unaccustomed frequency and regularity, and so had put on weight. He had received a variation on fan-mail: correspondence from clergymen, autograph-collectors, admiring maniacs, and people who were just plain puzzled by what he had done. (One of the last-mentioned category was Mr George Astley, proprietor of the high-class tobacco shop in Burlington Arcade, to whom Prince responded: 'Had Mr Terriss only spoken to me, he should have been alive now, and the poor Prince would have been in Scotland. He asked for it, and he got it. That's why I killed the cur who could only fight a gay woman[1] and a starving man. Sent on tour to ruin my character .... I must see a doctor. I should like one of the best in London. If you can do this for me God will reward you. My soul is all right .... Bring or send a white shirt and collars, 15 or 16, a tie, and

1. A reference that may have seeded a story that, with artistic deletions and additions, was told as if it were true for many years. In 1930, Harry Davis, the recently-retired manager of Rule's (already quoted, on page 22, some of his words in that instance being corroborated by other sources), gave his version of the story to the *Daily Herald*:

'At the Adelphi was a very charming and pretty girl, the daughter of an assistant stage carpenter named Prince. She used to tidy up the dressing-rooms every morning. One day when Terriss came in earlier than usual to collect his letters he found her in his room. Her freshness, charm and vivacity made an immediate appeal to the somewhat jaded senses of the actor.

'He began to make love to her – violent, passionate love that left the girl dazed and bewildered. His grace and gestures, his art, his voice, the commanding presence that was his, carried her off her feet.

'A few months later the girl had to leave the theatre. In her despair, she told her parents that the actor was to blame. The butterfly lover had flitted away in search of fresh flowers. That night Prince, the girl's father, tackled Terriss in the theatre. Burning rage against the betrayer of his daughter filled his heart and he reviled Terriss as no one had ever dared to revile the actor before.

'There was a violent quarrel. Terriss, in a fury, his vanity wounded and his conceit shaken, went to W. Brumsden, who was in charge of the stage hands, and demanded the dismissal of Prince that very minute. Prince was popular at the theatre. And he had justice on his side. But such was the power of Terriss, such was his voice in the affairs of the Adelphi, that Prince had to go. The Princes had suffered. The daughter had lost her good name; and the father had lost his job ....'

As the continuation of the story is tamely proximate to the real denouement, it can be left to moulder.

handkerchief, and one stud. I would ask my sister
Maggie again. She sent the last, but I don't think she is
in London. She sent me a lot of under-things last week
and ten shillings ....') As well as giving consideration to
his costume in the dock, he had decided, early on, to
assist his characterization with a beard of the Mephis-
tophelean kind. If it had occurred to him that he could,
on account of local prejudice, request a change of
venue for the trial, from the West End to some
provincial place, he had, one may safely assume, given
no second thought to an option that, if taken, might
result in his appearing in a forensic equivalent of the
Bijou Pavilion, Scunthorpe.

On the morning of the trial, London was smothered
by a pea-souper. The yellow-grey fog cloaked the tall
windows lining the wall to the left of the bench in the
principal court of the Old Bailey; intruding within, it
dwindled to a mist that, from the gallery, crowded with
people who had queued since the early hours, detri-
mentally to their lungs, gave the impression of a stage-
scene viewed through gauze.

Adding minutely to the feeling of theatricality, the
judge, Mr Justice Channell, sported a sparkling mono-
cle, and treated as a versatile prop – baton, italiciser,
toothbrush, ear-probe – the quill-pen that he seemed
rarely to use for its intended purpose. There was
nothing stagy about the leading prosecutor, Charles
Gill, senior counsel to the Treasury, who spoke with
an Irish brogue but often stumblingly, never with
eloquence or wit; epitomic of civil servants, he
appeared to wear wig and gown unwillingly, as if he
felt that they constituted a practical joke that tradition
should have known better than to play in a serious
place like a court of law.[1] Gill was assisted by Horace
Avory: twig-thin, his gown drooping from his shoul-

1.   Four weeks later, Gill was the prosecutor of Francis Carroll:
see footnote on page 43.

ders as if from a wire hanger, his features pursed to assemble an expression that in later years, when he was a judge, would help towards earning him the nickname of 'the acid-drop'. Avory's father had been Clerk of the Court at the Old Bailey, and his elder brother was the Clerk of Arraigns for the trial of Prince.

A Mr Sands and a Mr Kyd had been assigned to defend Prince. Neither of these barristers was (or ever would be) eminent. There was equality of numbers between the sides, prosecution and defence, but the imbalance of skills, of experience, was extreme. If any of the stage-people in the gallery whispered among themselves about the opposing castings, perhaps there was recollection of the brief tale of two actors, one famed for a tour de force, the other unknown and forced to tour.

Waiting for his call, Prince fretted that, as so often in the past, he was going to be let down by inadequate supporting players. Having made his escorted entrance through the trap in the floor of the dock, he gazed around the court, satisfying himself that he had drawn the town, and paid attention as Horace Avory's brother Kemp read the indictment and gave him his first cue, the question, 'Are you guilty or not guilty?'

'I am guilty – with provocation,' he replied. Then, turning his gaze towards the judge, he continued: 'I have to ask a favour. I believe the law of England allows an accused person the right to a Queen's Counsel. I have counsel, but I should like a Queen's Counsel to watch the case on my behalf.'

MR SANDS (*rising from his seat below the dock*): I am instructed, with my friend Mr Kyd, to defend the prisoner.

PRINCE (*affecting not to have noticed the interruption*): I understand that by the law of England I can have a Queen's Counsel. (*He lowers his head, his voice.*) I have no friends. My mother cannot help me with a penny for the defence. If you will not allow me to have it, I insist on saying that it must be paid by the people who drove me to do this crime.

MR JUSTICE CHANNELL (*quietly but firmly; dotting the air with his pen at full-stops*): You are not entitled by law to the services of a QC. On the contrary, if you desire the services of a QC, he would have to take out a licence to appear for you. You are entitled to have the benefit of counsel if you desire it. You are, of course, also entitled to defend yourself.

PRINCE: Thank you, my Lord.

MR JUSTICE CHANNELL (*indicating by his tone that he doubts the prisoner's ability to make wise decisions*): Assuming you are in a condition to indicate what you will do. (*He points his quill towards* MR SANDS.) There is a gentleman here who is prepared to conduct your case. I should advise you to accept his services.

PRINCE (*having had his attention distracted by the thought that it is some time since he groomed his rudimentary beard*): So long as I am allowed to defend myself, that is all I wish.

MR JUSTICE CHANNELL (*trying to be patient*): You cannot be allowed to defend yourself in a general way as well as being defended by counsel. You may be allowed to make a statement to the jury in addition to being defended by counsel. I shall allow that, but nothing more. You may suggest anything to counsel.

PRINCE: That is all I wish.

MR JUSTICE CHANNELL (*just to make sure*): Then you will be defended by counsel?

PRINCE (*certainly*): Certainly.

MR JUSTICE CHANNELL *taps the writing end of his quill on the bench to attract the notice of* THE CLERK OF ARRAIGNS, *and mutters at him to repeat*

> *the question regarding* PRINCE's *plea. This* THE
> CLERK OF ARRAIGNS *does.*
>
> PRINCE: I plead guilty – with the greatest
> provocation.
>
> MR JUSTICE CHANNELL (*less patiently*): You
> have told me you will be defended by counsel.
>
> PRINCE: Yes.
>
> MR JUSTICE CHANNELL: Then you had better
> take their advice before you plead.
>
> MR SANDS *and* MR KYD *rise and slant towards*
> PRINCE; *he leans over the wooden shelf of the
> dock toward them. There is a sotto-voce conversa-
> tion,* PRINCE *waving his Invernessed arms the
> while. Ultimately,* MR SANDS *and* MR KYD *subside,
> while* PRINCE *returns to an upright stance and
> addresses* MR JUSTICE CHANNELL.
>
> PRINCE: I have been advised to plead 'not
> guilty' – so I plead 'not guilty'.

The curtain-raiser over with, Charles Gill took little
more time to outline the case for the Crown. The first
prosecution witness was Tom Terriss. Examined by
Horace Avory, he said that he had last seen his father
alive on 15 Decemeber. The following night, shortly
before eleven o'clock, he had seen him lying dead at the
Adelphi. He did not know the prisoner.

> PRINCE: I saw you once during *The Harbour
> Lights*, in the dressing-room. Perhaps you will
> remember that.

Ralph Croyden, manager of Miss Lena Develrey's
London Theatrical Company, was called next. The
reporter for the *Daily Telegraph* noted that when he
came into the court,

> the unfortunate man in the dock squared his
> shoulders and assumed a histrionic smile, which
> was clearly intended to convey how little he
> thought of his quondam employer. This facial by-

play was continued through the witness's evidence. His statement that the accused described himself when he applied for employment as having played big parts at the Adelphi was the occasion for a confident glance at the jury. The sequel that Mr Croyden found that he could not play any part was met with a reproachful smile directed at the speaker. All this time the prisoner was busy with memoranda for his counsel, and he changed his position as the whim took him, now standing, now sitting. He had not tired yet of his miserable attempts to make an impression. The recall of his statement that 'The world would ring with his madness' was the signal for another quiet display of self-satisfaction, strangely incongruous with the awful position in which the verification of that prophesy had placed him.

Among the following witnesses were Charles Coltson (who, incidentally, had arranged for the briefing of a barrister to watch the proceedings on behalf of the Actors' Benevolent Fund); Charlotte Darby, Prince's landlady at Eaton Court; John Graves, and Constable Bragg.

At noon – by then, the fog had cleared from the streets, the mist from the court – Charles Gill announced that the case for the Crown was closed. After an adjournment, Mr Sands asked the jury 'to disabuse their minds of all that had been said outside, and to pretend ignorance of the sympathy that was felt at the loss of one whose name had become almost a household word'; having explained how, as it seemed to him, madness was defined by the law, he said that he was confident that the forthcoming evidence would convince the jury that Prince was insane.

The *Telegraph*'s man again:

For an hour and more the cultivated and polished accents of counsel and the rugged Doric of Dundonian witnesses were interwoven in comical medley. It was far from plain sailing for either side, differences of dialect leading to constant misunderstanding.

As Mrs Archer, the prisoner's mother, passed slowly towards the witness-box and climbed laboriously up its steps – she was old and frail – the fixed smile faded for a time from her son's face, his eyes shone brighter, and one was fain to hope that natural affection was not entirely gone from that strange mind.

The idea received a shock a few moments later. The poor old lady, who, it may be mentioned, suffered from extreme deafness, spoke in a very low voice, and on counsel complaining that they could not catch her words, her son shouted from the dock, 'Speak louder, Mother, they can't hear you.'

She was very Scotch, and very canny, referring counsel on one or two points to other witnesses with the remark, 'She'll tell you that,' but withal was ready to sacrifice her mother tongue to the vocabulary of the 'Southern English'. Prince was 'never right' from his birth, she said, and swiftly terminated a pause of puzzlement with the addendum, 'He was born mad.' When he was a baby, she had occasion to leave him in the harvest-field. When she came to him she found him blue in the face. He had received a sunstroke. Her son was 'dour to learn'; then she tried again with 'bad in the uptake,' and finally achieved success with 'slow at learning'. Her next problem in Scotch was more difficult. Speaking of the accused's bursts of rage, she said, 'They pit him rang in his mind, his passions.' Two jurymen by her side could not understand her, though she repeated the phrase more than once, and then the prisoner interposed, 'She said they put me wrong in the mind, my passions. That is the English of it.'

Speaking of times when he was unemployed and living with her, she said that he was sometimes not very well pleased; he used to think she doctored his food. He had told her a Mr Arthur had kept him from getting work in the Dundee Theatre, and in saying so he used the word 'blackmailing'. This was eight years ago. He had told her he himself was the Lord Jesus Christ and that she was the Virgin Mary, and had charged her with adulterating his tea. When he was affected with what she described as 'his turns', he would sing songs and hymns, and his eyes would stare out of his head. He had left Dundee for the last time five months ago. His father was formerly married, and a son by that marriage was mad from his birth but never locked up: he was silly.

Other Dundonians spoke of Prince's oddities of behaviour. And so did Arthur Ellison, the manager of a theatre at Southport, in Lancashire, who recalled: 'While in my employ, and afterwards, I received postcards from him which spoke of blackmailing and horse-whipping. He charged me with thwarting him in getting an engagement, and called me a hell-hound.'

PRINCE: Shut up! Shut up!
WITNESS: If I am not mistaken, I discharged him.
PRINCE: If I am not mistaken, you are wrong.
MR GILL: He had a very exalted opinion of his powers?
WITNESS: Actors in his position usually have.
MR GILL: Can you remember a particular part he played?
WITNESS: The sergeant who led on the soldiers.
PRINCE (*provoked by sniggers from the gallery*): It was a very good part.

The final witnesses were doctors: the medical officer at Holloway Gaol, who said that he had paid close attention to Prince during his stay, and two 'experts in lunacy', both of whom admitted to Charles Gill that their evidence was based chiefly on their observations of the prisoner's demeanour in the dock. The three were unanimous in the opinion that Prince had been mad when he murdered, and was still. When one of the specialists remarked that 'a person of sound mind would display, or at least feign, remorse at having committed such a dreadful deed', Prince cried out: 'Why should I? Terriss blackmailed me for ten years.'

After the closing speeches, the first for the defence, neither lasting more than a quarter of an hour, Mr Justice Channell summed up, and at 6.30 the jury retired to consider their verdict.

Shortly before the trial, Henry Irving had told a friend: 'They will find some excuse to get Prince off – mad or something,' and had added what he considered an explanation: 'Terriss was an actor, so his murderer will not be executed.'

Whatever Irving meant by that last comment, his prophesies were made true at seven o'clock, when the foreman of the jury announced that 'although the prisoner knew what he was doing and whom he was doing it to, upon the medical evidence he was not responsible for his actions'.

Prince's look of puzzlement was replaced by a broad smile as the judge explained the import of the verdict: 'that the prisoner shall be confined in a criminal lunatic asylum until Her Majesty's pleasure to be known,'

'Shall I be allowed to make any thanks to the Court for that?' Prince asked – and, without waiting for a reply, went on: 'I should like to thank the gentlemen who have assisted me in the case. Of course, I did not bring my defence properly forward after the medical evidence, because I did not think it necessary. I will only say that I have had a very fair trial.'

'I cannot allow any statement,' Mr Justice Channell snapped. 'You had better not make any.'

'Well, the only thing I can say, my Lord, is that I thank you very much.'

'That is all.' Without further ado, Mr Justice Channell turned his pen into a wand, and Richard Archer Prince was made to disappear.

He spent the next thirty-nine years, the rest of his life, in the Broadmoor Criminal Lunatic Asylum. There, he was accorded celebrity status. Not because of the act that had resulted in his confinement. And not, as you might have thought, because he filched all the star parts in productions by the Broadmoor dramatic society. Giving up acting in favour of musicianship, he appointed himself conductor of the inmates' orchestra. He had a fine time, waving his baton with great panache, gesticulating, shouting things like *apassionato* and *agitato*, and every so often looking over his shoulder to see how the audience was responding to his performance. Marringly for many, the concerts lacked concertedness. Each of the instrumentalists played a different tune, and none took the slightest notice of the man who had once dreamed of being The Prince of Players.

Shooting Script

Once upon a time before movies were made to talk, there were three females stars, each described as 'the public's sweetheart'. Their names were given more prominence on billboards than the productions in which they appeared; gossip columnists publicized their every (well, almost every) off-set action, quoted what their press agents claimed to be quotes from the goddesses, and transmuted into a Revelation anything the sweethearts, goddesses, stars of the silver screen, or whatever they were being called, had written, even if it was only a shopping-list or a note saying no to an invitation.

But as celebrities go, they went. Now they are virtually forgotten except by old-movie addicts ... and devotees of true crime. *Edna Purviance* is a name that may ring a bell in your mind – chiefly because it crops up among the credit titles of many Charlie Chaplin pictures. And there's *Mabel Normand* – probably remembered, if at all, as Roscoe 'Fatty' Arbuckle's co-star in a series of comedies that frequently had their slim plots contorted so as to allow a scene or two featuring Mack Sennett's bathing beauties, daringly showing off their chubby knees. But what of *Mary Miles Minter*? Have you heard of her? Assuming that you haven't, let me tell you that in early 1922, when she was still only seventeen, she was perhaps the most popular of all the female stars; according to one 'filmologist', she had 'even passed Mary Pickford in the esteem of the fans.'

Some of Mary Miles Minter's greatest successes, including the film of *Anne of Green Gables*, were directed by William Desmond Taylor.

During the investigation into the murder of Mr Taylor at his Hollywood home on the night of Wednesday, 1 February 1922, Miss Minter's name was near the top of the list of possible culprits. And so were those of Mabel Normand and Edna Purviance.

I can think of no other murder case with such a star-studded cast. And I have to rack my brains for a case more likely to be turned down as the scenario of a film on account of its being too bizarre to be believed.

Take, for instance, the background of the victim. William Desmond Taylor was a real mystery man. To start with, his name was actually William Cunningham Deane-Tanner. The son of a major in the British Army, he was born at the family home on the Bellevue Estates in County Cork, Ireland, in 1877. A brother, called Dennis – another mystery man, as you will find out – was born a year later. When, in their late teens, both brothers ignored their father's order that they must follow in his military footsteps, he sent them packing. Perhaps together, perhaps separately, they travelled to America. William, so it is said, prospected for gold, first in Colorado, then in the Klondike, lastly in Montana, but in none of those places to his profit.

By the turn of the century, he was the manager of an establishment entitled the English Antique Shop at 240 Fifth Avenue, Manhattan. In December 1901, he married Ethel May Harrison, the daughter of a stockbroker; some accounts have it that she was one of the original Floradora girls, but that is said of so many women whose names crop up in accounts of American murder cases of the first quarter of this century that, if all the attributions are correct, there must have been more pretty maidens on the stage of the Casino Theatre, Manhattan, on the night of 10 November 1900 than there were people in the auditorium. The likelihood that Ethel was, or had been, connected with the stage in some way, not necessarily Floradorally, is strengthened by the fact that the wedding was held at the Little Church Around the Corner, which is the 'actors' church' of New York City, the equivalent of St Paul's in London's Covent Garden. The couple settled down in the outlying, and the fashionable, town of Larchmont, and in 1903 had a child, a daughter, whom they named Ethel Daisy.

Now, at last, one can be precise about a time and a date. At noon on 23 October 1908, William walked out of the antique shop, saying that he was taking an early lunch. He didn't return that day. Next morning, he telephoned the shop from an hotel, asking for $600 to be sent to him by messenger. The cash was delivered – and, without a word to anyone, not even his wife or his five-year-old daughter, William Cunningham Deane-Tanner vanished.

Four years later, his wife divorced him on the ground that he had committed adultery before his disappearance. Shortly before the decree was made absolute, William's brother Dennis also vanished, leaving a wife and two children, and causing the owner of the antique shop on Fifth Avenue where he had worked (not the one that had suddenly lost the services of William) to carry out an unscheduled inventory of the stock and an audit of the accounts; nothing showed up to suggest why Dennis had left without giving notice.

What the brothers did soon after each had, as some Americans are wont to say, 'taken a powder', is anyone's guess. Did Dennis join up with William? No one knows.

But some five years after leaving New York, William turned up in Hollywood, which was fast becoming the movie capital of the world. Calling himself William Desmond Taylor, he found acting jobs.

Back on the east coast, his ex-wife, now remarried, happened to see a film in which he played a small part; there was no mistaking his thin, chiselled features, his charming smile, his rather flamboyant gestures. Later in the day, she informed Dennis's ex-wife (yes, she, too, had obtained a divorce) of the shock she had had in the cinema. Whether because of this news or for some unrelated reason, the woman deserted by Dennis soon afterwards packed her belongings and moved to a small town not far from Hollywood. She got in touch with William, who was now a film-director. Though he refused to admit his true identity, he put her on his mailing list to receive $50 a month – enclosing with each payment a note saying that she was a total stranger to him.

By the time America entered the war against the Germans, William Desmond Taylor was the senior director in the Famous Players-Lasky Co. He threw up his job to fight the foe. As he had never applied for naturalization, he joined a Canadian regiment. Following initial training, he was sent to England – but by then the Armistice had been signed. He was posted back to Canada in the summer of 1919, and shortly after being promoted to the rank of captain, was demobilized.

Returning to Hollywood, he negotiated a contract as a director at the Paramount studios. Unlike most of the leading lights of the film colony, he lived simply in a small, tastefully-furnished house. Subsequent to the murder, Mabel Normand said that 'Bill's house was part of an attractive arrangement. There were eight little two-storey cottages built round a U, three on each side and two at the end, the open end of the U fronting on [South] Alvarado Street. The second house on the left was occupied by Edna Purviance, the third was Bill Taylor's, and the last one on the right was rented by Douglas MacLean and his wife.' (MacLean was a film-actor who specialized in high-society roles.)

Taylor employed only one full-time servant – called a valet, but in fact a jack-of-several-trades, responsible for keeping the house tidy, purchasing food and drink, preparing the former for the table and mixing the latter into cocktails, dealing with routine correspondence, and looking after his master's two cars, paying special heed to the custom-built MacFarland convertible. Until late in 1921, when Taylor travelled to England to receive treatment for a stomach-ulcer, the valet was an Englishman known as Edward Sands. Yet another enigmatic figure in the case. The relationship between Taylor and Sands has never been clarified. It is known that Sands had served in the British Army during the Great War – and that at that time he was using the name of Edward Fitz-Strathmore. While Taylor was in England in the autumn of 1921, Sands, or whatever his name was, seems to have run amok: he forged Taylor's signature on a number of cheques, pawned his employer's jewellery, stole his clothes, and wrecked his second-best car. Perhaps needless to say, he was not at the house when Taylor returned. He was never seen again – a fact that would encourage one journalist to refer to him as 'Shifting Sands', and another, more venturesome, to comment that 'Sands had run out'.

Taylor hired a man named Henry Peavey as Sands' replacement. Whereas Sands was enigmatic, Peavey was ... well, let's say that he was strange. A diminutive Negro, he was extravagantly homosexual, falsetto-voiced, sway-hipped, and larger than lady-like in the way he flapped the scented air around him with his hands, the nails of which sparkled like splinters of pink-tinctured glass. Henry was addicted to drugs, and was nimble with needles of a different kind – those that he used in his spare-time pursuits of embroidering and crocheting. Don't run away with the idea that, because Taylor had a homosexual servant, he too was homosexual. Nothing could be farther from the truth. To quote an acquaintance: 'There is no denying that William Desmond Taylor was no St Anthony in his relations with scatter-brained maidens.'

But more about that side of his life later. For the moment, let me return to Henry Peavey – just to say that it was he who found the dead body of the film director. It gave him quite a turn. In his own words:

'I turned back-to-front and run out of the house and yelled. And then I yelled some more.'

The penultimate person to see Taylor alive – or to put it another way, the person who, without much choice in the matter, admitted to being the last to have had social intercourse with him before he was murdered – was Mabel Normand.

Referred to by most gossip-columnists as 'Madcap Mabel', and by an exceptionally inventive one as 'the playgirl of the western world', her life was as hectic as any of the comedies in which she appeared. Even by Hollywood's standards, her behaviour was unconventional (on one occasion, at an alfresco party, she berated a man for making 'indecent suggestions', then took off all her clothes and dived into the pool), and she used her own money as if she were a socialist using someone else's (as an example, she couldn't be bothered to set her watch backwards or forwards when travelling between time-zones, and so she carried a collection of watches with different settings, replacing one with another as she travelled, throwing away those that were no longer correct).

She had a long-running love-affair with Mack Sennett, the head of the studio to which she was contracted, but this came to an end – abruptly – when she walked into his apartment and found Sennett wearing only his underpants, and the actress Mae Busch (who later achieved fame as one of the 'angry wives' in the Laurel and Hardy movies) wearing only a loose-fitting charm-bracelet. Mabel refused to accept Sennett's explanation that he was tutoring Miss Busch for a production entitled *A One-Night Stand*.

Soon after that incident, Mabel met William Desmond Taylor. They took to each other at once, and what reporters delicately called a 'deep friendship' developed. Exemplifying the notion that comedians dream of playing Hamlet, Mabel nurtured an ambition to switch from slapstick to drama. Taylor, believing that she could succeed as a serious actress, did his best to 'refine' her, taking her to see what he considered worth-while films and plays, and suggesting books she should read. As Taylor was not only a leading director but also president of the prestigious Motion Picture Directors' Association, Mabel's intimacy with him made headlines – confusing ones at times, leaving readers to try to fathom how someone dubbed 'Madcap Mabel' could be a 'serious-minded star'.

According to Mabel's version of events on Wednesday, 1 February 1922, she got up at midday and, having nothing more pressing to do, flipped through the pages of a couple of books that Taylor had lent her: one volume, presumably intended to improve her mind, was all about Freudian theories, while the other was Ethel M. Dell's swelteringly romantic novel *The Rocks of Valpré*, which Taylor had suggested might be adapted to the screen.

Later in the afternoon, she sorted through the many gifts of jewellery that she had received at Christmas from friends and fans. 'I decided to load my car with these things and go to various jewellers, where I could exchange some and have the others engraved. So I had William Davis, my chauffeur, carry the packages out to the car, and then I scurried into my clothes and we set off.'

It was getting on towards seven o'clock when she finished her errands. She telephoned her apartment and received two messages from Mamie Owens, her maid. The studio had called to say that she was needed for location-work early the next morning. And Taylor had rung to say that he had two more books for her.

'I told Mamie I would drive by Bill Taylor's place and come on home. I started to step into my car, and suddenly felt a great appetite for peanuts. I bought two bags and one of popcorn. Then we went on to Bill's house. I told Willliam Davis I'd only be a little while, and asked him to sweep out the peanut shells I'd scattered all over the floor of the car. I walked up the left-hand walk to Bill's little house. I carried a bag of peanuts to show my gratitude for the two books he had for me.

'When I reached Bill's open door, I heard a voice inside: he was using the telephone. I walked around the flower-beds a few minutes until he had quit talking and hung up. Whoever it was calling him seemed intensely absorbed in what he had to say. As soon as he had hung up, I rang his bell.

' "Hello, Mabel darling," he said. "I know what you've come for – the books." '

' "Righto, my bright duck," I said, going in.'

Taylor offered her dinner, but she declined, explaining about the early-morning location-call. She said she had time for a drink.

After shouting to Henry Peavey to mix a cocktail, Taylor pointed to his writing-table, which was littered with cancelled cheques, income-tax forms, and bank statements. 'If the police ever find Edward Sands,' he said, 'you can bet I'll do plenty to him.' He went on, more explicitly: 'Nearly every one of the cheques on that table is a forgery – and, do you know, Sands did such a good job that, to save my life, I can't tell which are my signatures and which are duds. I'm going mad. I don't think I'll ever get it sorted out.'

Peavey swayed in, carrying Emerald Ladies on a silver salver that his predecessor had left behind. 'How do you do, Miss Normand?' he inquired. 'I trust all is well with you.'

'All's well, Henry, thanks,' Mabel replied. (In her account, she interpolated the information that 'Henry had been released from jail that morning, Bill having gone down to get him out of some trouble he'd got into.' She added that, as soon as Peavey had served the drinks, Taylor told him that he could go home: 'Henry fluttered about a while, and then bowed as he went out, leaving the door open as he always did. It was about twenty minutes after seven. Henry left each evening after dinner and came the next morning soon after seven.')

Left alone, Taylor and Mabel chatted for a few minutes. As Mabel got up to go, he gave her the books, the heavier of which was by Nietzsche.

'He said he'd telephone me at nine o'clock, and I said, all right, but that Mamie wouldn't disturb me if I'd gone to sleep by then. He walked down towards the street with me. When we reached the kerb, my chauffeur was standing at the door of my car, his feet in the peanuts shells. Bill helped me into the car, and I was driven away. I looked back, and we wafted kisses on our hands to each other as long as I could see him standing there on the sidewalk.

'I never saw him again. And he didn't telephone me at nine o'clock, as he had promised, for he was lying on the floor of his living-room, shot through the back and dead within a few minutes after I left him.

Before explaining how Mabel Normand was aware of the approximate time of the murder, let me tell you about the discovery of the crime.

At seven o'clock on the morning after Mabel's visit, Henry Peavey arrived at the house to start work. As soon as he opened the door and entered the living-room, he saw the body of William Desmond Taylor stretched out on the carpet. An overturned chair was lying across the legs.

It seems more likely that Henry thought his employer had been taken ill than that he realized that he was dead. In any event, the valet rushed out into the U-shaped courtyard and started yelling.

In no time at all, several neighbours in various states of undress were staring through the open doorway. The neighbours included Edna Purviance, who lived next door and Douglas MacLean, the player of dinner-jacketed parts, whose house was directly opposite Taylor's.

If for no other reason, the Taylor murder case deserves to be recorded in the annals of crime because of the tidiness of the victim. The body looked as if it had been laid out; the legs were exactly parallel, the feet towards the door, and the arms appeared, as one observer noted, 'to be in the "at-attention" position – only horizontal'. The jacket was not at all rumpled, and the collar and tie were impeccably neat. There was no sign of injury.

Indeed, the death seemed so natural that the first doctor to arrive ascribed it to heart disease. Not until a coroner put in an appearance and, no respecter of tidiness in cases of sudden death, turned the body over, was it seen that Taylor had been shot. A .38–calibre bullet of obsolete design had entered the left side of the back, near the bottom of the rib-cage, and travelled diagonally upwards, coming to rest just below the skin on the right-hand side of the neck.

Confusingly, the holes made by the bullet in the clothing did not match up: with the arms at the sides, the hole in the jacket was some inches lower than the one in the waistcoat.

Peculiar, that. But no more so than other aspects of the crime which would perplex the investigators infuriatingly over the next days, weeks, months.

When Edna Purviance learned of the death of her next-door neighbour, she made two telephone calls, both to lady-friends of the deceased.

One of the calls was to Mary Miles Minter. The blonde-ringletted star became hysterical. She ran to-wards the front door, intending to drive over to South Alvarado Street to perform an unscripted variation on the girl-with-dying-loved-one scenes she had played in the last reels of innumerable weepies. But she was dragged back by her formidable mother Charlotte Shelby (the star's real name – and it is hard to understand why she discarded it – was Juliet Shelby). After some argument – during which, according to an eavesdropping maid, Mrs Shelby asked but received no reply to the question, 'And where were you last night?' – Miss Minter collapsed into a chair. Happening to catch a glimpse of herself in one of the many mirrors, she abruptly stopped whimpering.

'Look, Mother,' she said excitedly – 'look at my expression. Don't I register frozen horror to perfection?'

'Hold it, dear,' her mother said, running behind her to peek at the reflected expression. For a while they chatted about how she could make use of the expression in a movie.

But as it turned out, the Taylor murder case put an end to Mary Miles Minter's film career. During searches of the director's house, the police found, first of all, a silk nightgown bearing a 3–M monogram, and subsequently a letter on perfumed notepaper emblazoned with the self-same monogram, which read: 'Dearest – I love you – I love you – I love you –.' This repetitive message was followed by a surfeit of kiss-crosses and the words, 'Yours always – Mary.' The publicity given to these items so tarnished Mary Miles Minter's image (a spiteful rival commented, 'So now we know she picked that middle-name to show how far she's willing to go') that her studio rescinded her contract – paying her a large sum, perhaps a million dollars, for the right to do so. She came to Europe (and her mother came, too), and so relished the cuisine that she was distinctly unsylphlike when she returned home. Despite her attempts to convince the press and the once-adoring public that she had been secretly betrothed to William Desmond Taylor and that if the murder had been postponed for a week or two, she would now be a widow, she never got a further chance to register frozen horror – or any other emotion, for that matter – on the silver screen. She and her mother moved into a mansion in Santa Monica. Mrs Shelby socialized, but Mary, growing chubbier as the years went by, lived almost reclusively, her rare jaunts usually being for the purpose of viewing property that she had bought or was thinking of buying. As soon as Mrs Shelby died, in 1957, Mary married a business associate with the cosmopolitan name of O'Hildebrandt. He died in 1965; she, at the age of eighty-two, from heart failure, in August 1984.

The other telephone call made by Edna Purviance was to Mabel Normand, who was sitting in her apartment, made-up and dressed in a sort of Spanish costume, complete with black-lace mantilla, waiting for her chauffeur to arrive to drive her out of town for location-shooting. Just like Miss Minter, Mabel exhibited hysterics. Also like Miss Minter, she calmed down very quickly. Showing that her label of 'Madcap Mabel' was not altogether appropriate, she thought things through – then, still in the sort of Spanish togs (but without the mantilla, which might hide her face in press photographs), she told her chauffeur to drive her to South Alvarado Street, stepping on the gas.

Did Edna Purviance make a third telephone call? It seems likely, for when Mabel arrived at William Desmond Taylor's house, at about the same time as the police, studio executives were rummaging around in search of association items that might damage the repute of stars who had been his guests. Mabel, as we know, had been a frequent visitor – indeed, she had been at the house only the night before, leaving soon after 7.30.

Just as well for her, evidence turned up to show that Taylor was alive when she left. A resident of one of the houses facing the U-shaped courtyard had been sitting by his window: he had seen Mabel walking to her car, accompanied by Taylor – and, more important, had

seen the film-director retracing his steps after blowing
kisses until her car turned the corner. Slight corroboration of this eye-witness testimony was provided by
peanut shells, which partly outlined where the car had
been parked.

It seemed clear that the murder was committed at
least a quarter of an hour later. Douglas MacLean
recalled that, at about eight o'clock, there was 'a
shattering report – muffled yet penetrating'; and his
wife not only remembered the explosion but said that
she had at once gone to the verandah and had seen 'a
short, stocky man, with a scarf round his neck and his
cap pulled down, come out of Taylor's cottage, close
the door carefully behind him, glance casually about,
and then disappear into an alley beside the cottage'.

Checking through recent reports of crimes, so far
unsolved, in the vicinity, the police noted that Taylor's
house had been broken into on two occasions during
the winter. There had been a most peculiar aftermath to
the crimes: Taylor had received in the mail an envelope
containing pawn-tickets for some of the loot – pawn-
tickets made out in the name of William Deane-
Tanner. It was possible, of course, that the burglar who
was so thoughtful after the events had come across a
document showing his victim's real name while looking for things to take. On the other hand, maybe he
had had this baptismal information prior to his first
illegal entry. That possibility led to another, and that to
a third: perhaps the burglar was the director's former
valet Edward Sands ... and perhaps the name of
'Edward Sands' had masked the true identity of a valet
who wasn't a valet at all but was actually the director's
long-lost brother Dennis.

Charmed by their piling of possibilities, the police
asked Mrs MacLean whether the man she had seen
leaving Taylor's house could have been Sands. 'Definitely not,' she replied. A mite crestfallen at the
demolition of the pointing spire above the three storeys

very sincerely you
W. Terriss

Terriss as Julian Peveril

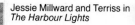
Jessie Millward and Terriss in
The Harbour Lights

Assasination of William Terriss

William Desmond Taylor

Mabel Normand

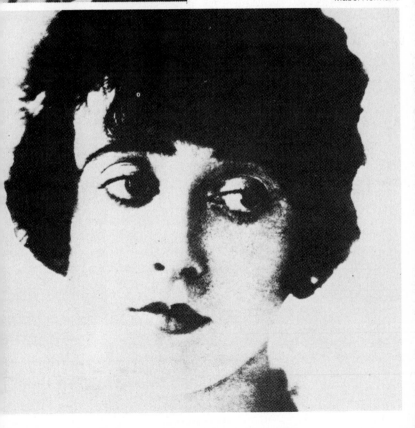

Mary Miles Minter

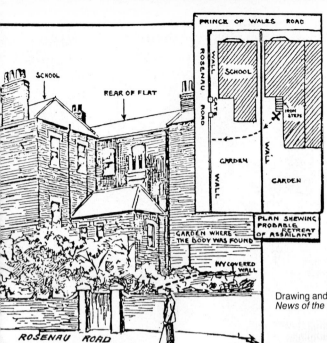

PLAN SHEWING PROBABLE RETREAT OF ASSAILANT

Drawing and plan from the
News of the World

Fatty Arbuckle

Virginia Rappe

(above) PEACE ENTERTAINS HIS FRIENDS
Taken from Charles Peace: or, *The Adventures of a
Notorious Burglar,* published by G. Purkess,
London, no date (circa 1900)

(right) Charles Peace

(opposite right) Gr ucho Marx and Thelma Todd

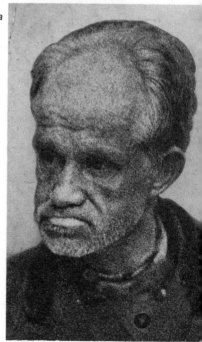

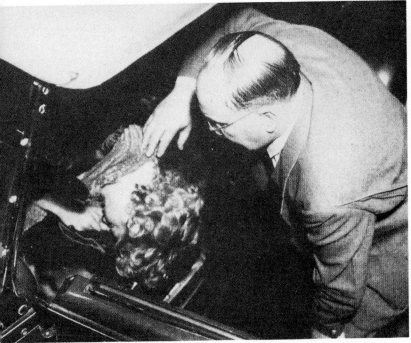

A homicide detective perusing Thelma Todd's body

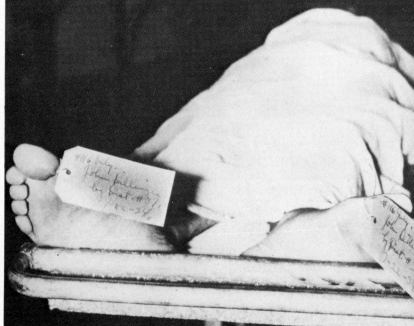

(above) The Biograph Theatre one hour after Dillinger's Shooting (below) Dillinger's body alone in the morgue awaiting the embalmer

of conjecture, the police raised a separate idea. Was it conceivable, they inquired of Mrs MacLean, that the person she had observed was a woman in male clothing? After reflecting a moment, frowning her memory into focus, she said yes: 'the stranger *was* built more like a woman than a man.'

The testimony of the window-seated witness seemed to rule out Mabel Normand as a suspect. Still, when she arrived at the house following receipt of Edna Purviance's telephone call, she had cause to be worried: she had lavished upon Taylor autographic indications of her affection for him, and if unbridled examples became exhibits, her nickname of 'Madcap Mabel' might lose favour to 'Sex-mad Normand', which would never do. Knowing precisely where certain of her letters were kept – in a chest of drawers in Taylor's bedroom – she dashed upstairs and opened the drawers: only to discover that the letters were not there.

Now, here is another oddity – similar, in a way, to those pawn-tickets that were posted to Taylor. A few days later, Mabel was given the letters. Just who gave them to her – a detective or a studio mogul who had looked through them and decided that they were inoffensive – was something that she never divulged. Among Mabel-associated items left in the house and referred to by the investigators were three pictures of her, each with a fulsome salutation, on the walls of the room where Taylor was found dead; a locket holding a photograph of her, this inscribed, 'To My Dearest'; and – fished from the depths of a wellington boot, a hidey-hole that had escaped the notice of the pre-investigation investigators – a bundle of letters in Mabel's hand, one addressed to 'Dearest Daddy' and signed 'Blessed Baby'. Mabel's connection with the Taylor case did her no harm at all: it may even have added spice to her saucy image, making her an even bigger box-office draw. (However, within a few years her popularity began to wane; her rackety way of life started to take its toll. She died from consumption in 1930.)

The police could have done without some of the 'help' they received from the public, once the case hit the headlines. As well as thousands of letters and telegrams suggesting clues and voicing suspicions, there were 300 confessions to the crime – most, of course, from native sensation-seekers, but some from people in Great Britain who hoped to 'get in on the act'. Rumours were rife about the motive for the murder – and a few of the rumours either sprang from facts or collected factual support during their travels. An examination of Taylor's bank statements revealed several series of regular withdrawals of cash (nothing to do with the monthly stipend to his brother's ex-wife, which was paid by cheque; commencing prior to Edward Sand's arrival and continuing after his departure; separate from withdrawals to cover everyday expenses). Was he being blackmailed? If so, why? Could it be that some or all of the apparent instalment-payments were in aid of silence about aspects of his love-life? (Henry Peavey spoke of a pink nightgown that was kept irrelevantly in a desk-drawer: according to the valet, he had a 'distinctive' way of folding 'garments of material that won't hold still' – and on 'many occasions' he found that the folds in the gown were indistinctive, indicating that it had been used and afterwards carefully, but not quite carefully enough, arranged into an appearance of non-use.) Talk of blackmail meant that the name of Edward Sands again cropped up in discussion. Was Sands – ex-Edward Fitz-Strathmore – actually Dennis Deane-Taylor? Come to think of it, Taylor had seemed more irritated than furious over the mess left, forgeries perpetrated, and valuables stolen by the vanished valet: he had not given the impression of being keen to have the miscreant apprehended and prosecuted.

Turning the suspicion of blackmail on its head, the police wondered whether Taylor had been killed by someone *he* was blackmailing. Proponents of this notion were intrigued by a bunch of keys found in the buttoned back-pocket of Taylor's trousers: the keys fitted none of the doors that a detective tried them in. Were they keys to cupboards or deposit-boxes that held proofs of secrets learned and put to financial advantage by Taylor?

Or did the motive for the murder have something to do with drugs? Two possible answers were bandied. One had it that, because Taylor had spoken out strongly against the prevalence of drug-takers in the film industry, a trafficker had decided to protect his business interests; the other suggested that Taylor was himself a pusher and that he had been 'rubbed out' by a client or a rival.

There were any number of other theories. The police followed up some of them – but each led either to a dead-end or to a wall of silence erected by bosses of studios.

Added together, a few facts and unanswered questions point waveringly towards a possible murderer. Or rather, murderess.

Remembering that the body looked as if it had been 'laid out' – millimetrically symmetrical, hardly a single unfashioned crease marring the sartorial perfection – is it possible that Taylor was slain by a lady-friend who had discovered that she was one among many (none of the rest being publicized as friends by having their inscribed pictures displayed on the living-room wall) and who, after murdering from revenge, from jealousy, or for no better reason than that she was piqued by Taylor's disinclination to allow that she was his star, the others mere supporting performers, still worshipped him to the extent that she wanted him to make a presentable corpse?

Another question – apparently small but perhaps

salient – arises from Mabel Normand's statement that when she arrived at the house to collect a couple of books from Taylor, he was speaking on the phone to someone who had *called him* and who was '*intensely absorbed*' in what he was saying. How on earth did she know either of these things if, as she said, Taylor was already on the phone when she arrived and she waited in the garden, munching peanuts, until he hung up? If there was such a person as The Absorbed Caller, he or she preferred to remain anonymous, despite repeated pleas from the police, headlined in the press, that he or she should come forward. The timidity was understandable, considering that many people equated absorption with grave concern, and assumed that as soon as the caller had replaced the receiver, he or she had hastened to South Alvarado Street for the express purpose, as a reporter picturesquely put it, 'of breaking Mr Taylor's connection with Life'.

There was a conflict between the evidence of William Davis, Mabel's chauffeur, and that of a studio technician. The latter said that he had seen Davis near Taylor's house on the night of the murder: he couldn't be sure of the time of the sighting, but was certain that it was *not* around 7.30, when Davis was uncontroversially adjacent to the courtyard, waiting for Mabel.

By New Year's Eve, 1923 – twenty-three months after the murder – Mabel had a different chauffeur, Horace Greer. Curtailing a party attended by Mabel and Edna Purviance, Horace fired a pistol at the host, a millionaire named Courtland Q. Dines. Surgeons managed to save Dines's life, but it was a close-run thing. When the case came to court, he was physically fit – but, so he said, 'still sick' insofar as his recollection of the party was concerned. Mabel was not in court – indeed, not even in California. She had 'gone on an unprearranged trip'. The district attorney refused to proceed without her presence, and eventually the chauffeur was acquitted.

Was Mary Miles Minter telling the truth when she said that she and Taylor were secretly engaged, imminent of matrimony? Could Mabel Normand have learnt of the liaison, the intention to make it proper? Was she the 'man' wearing a cap and scarf who was seen by Mrs Douglas MacLean directly after the shooting? One can only say 'perhaps' to all those questions.

Was she responsible for the still-unsolved crime? Again, one can only say 'perhaps' – adding that it was just the sort of madcap, spur-of-the-moment thing she *might* have done. If she had been cast as the Killer in a screen version of the case, she would have had audiences rolling about in the aisles – particularly when, at the close of the pivotal shooting/tidying-the-body scene, she stood pigeon-toed, an over-large cap worn Jackie-Coogan-style, a scarf bearding her chin, and mouthed 'Ho-hum' at the camera before shrugging away her naughtiness and making a comical exit.

Death in Carpet-Slippers

The longer one studies murder cases, the more one *expects* to come across stranger-than-fiction coincidences – either within particular cases or as fortuities that deflect the mind from consideration of one case to recollection of another or others. Odd coincidences crop up so often that persons of a superstitious turn of mind might well conclude, brooking no argument from logicians, that murder can be contagious.

I suppose the oddest coincidence of all – the odds against it being a centillion or so to one – arose in Brighton in the summer of 1934. So-called trunk crimes, bodies treated as baggage, were rare in England: only a couple had come to light since 1831, when John Holloway, a resident of Brighton, had committed what was said to be the first of such crimes. But subsequent to Derby Day of 1934, the south-coast resort became known as The Queen of the Slaughtering Places by virtue of the fact that three cases – and I wish I hadn't had to use that word – were discovered in or within a stone's throw of the left-luggage office at the central railway station. The crimes had been committed independently, and the police, trying to unconfuse themselves and the public, decided to ignore one of the finds – the body of a baby – and to dub the others respectively 'Brighton Trunk Crime No. 1' and 'Brighton Trunk Crime No. 2'. Officially, at any rate, neither of the crimes was ever solved.

One of the settings of a less well-known coincidence was the Euston Palace of Varieties, which stood imposingly at the junction of Euston Road and Tonbridge Street, directly opposite St Pancras Railway Station. In January 1907, during a strike of music-hall

performers in aid of better pay and conditions, the
manager of the Palace announced his intention to
cobble together a bill of blacklegs. A prompt volunteer
was Dr Crippen's wife Cora, who went by the stage-
name of Belle Elmore. She can hardly be said to have
broken ranks with the strikers, for in the past ten years,
since her arrival from America, she had had precious
few opportunities to inflict her soprano voice on
paying audiences. A legend has it that when there was
talk of trying to stop her from crossing the picket-line
surrounding the stage-door of the Palace, Marie Lloyd
told fellow-strikers: 'Don't be daft. Let her in, and
she'll empty the house.' Belle Elmore's contributions
did not have that drastic effect, but by all accounts[1] she
usually made her exit to the sound of one hand
clapping. Afterwards, a backstage worker remembered
that

> she sang a song called 'Down Lovers' Walk' and
> also a coon song. She wore a short, spangled
> dress. She also sang a costume-song called 'The
> Major' and appeared in a musical dualogue[2]
> entitled 'The Unknown Quantity'. In one of the
> scenes she had to hold a sheaf of £5 notes. Dr
> Crippen's desire for realism was so great that he
> gave her a bundle of genuine notes which she left

1.   One of which has the incident occurring at the Bedford
Palace of Varieties in Camden High Street, half a mile or so south
of the Crippens' home at 39 Hilldrop Crescent, in the Holloway
district of North London. Since Belle occasionally sub-titled
herself 'La Belle Americaine', it seems likely that she teamed up
with another blackleg chantress, to make 'Les Belles Americaines,' an act advertised as appearing midway down the bill at
the Bedford in the week starting on Monday, 28 January 1907;
mass picketing on the Monday caused both of the twice-nightly
performances to be cancelled, but business was usual at the
Bedford for the rest of the week.

2.   Les Belles Americaines?

on the stage the first night. Fortunately, they were seen and handed to her.

Another of the turns on the bill was a performer who called himself Thomas Weldon Atherston. A 'resting' legitimate actor, he recited monologues – 'The Green Eye of the Little Yellow God,' ''Twas Christmas Day in the Workhouse': that sort of thing – while yobs in the pit and gallery, unappreciative of his sonorous voice, of the sentiments expressed in his rhymed tales, made up words of their own.

Both Belle Elmore and Thomas Weldon Atherston had an unhappy week at the Bedford. It would be nice to think that they tried to console each other, perhaps over a bottle of stout.

Three and a half years later, in the second week of July 1910, they shared top billing on the front page of just about every newspaper in the land.

Neither was able to savour the publicity.

The reason why Belle Elmore was in the news was that portions of her body, separated by her husband, had been found in the cellar of 39 Hilldrop Crescent, while the sudden celebrity of Thomas Weldon Atherston was all because – but no; it will be best, I think, if I tell you something of his background before explaining the circumstances that made him newsworthy.

'Atherston' was his stage-name, his real one being Anderson. Perhaps when he started as an actor – that would have been round about 1883, when he was twenty – there was already a Thomas Anderson treading the boards, and he decided to make the slight change to his name so as to avoid confusion. So far as I can tell, he never appeared in the West End; but in the early years, at any rate, he was kept busy as a character actor in touring productions, usually of melodramas.

Even allowing for the fact that it was only the unconventional nature of his demise that earned him an obituary in the stage-paper *The Era*, one feels that the

obituarist should have troubled himself to learn more about his subject, or, failing that, added a few details – dates and places – to what he did write,
which was this:

> Mr Atherston was a quiet, reserved man, and a sound and useful actor. His best impersonation was that of Richard, Duke of Gloucester, in *Jane Shore*,[1] but he played heavy leads in Mr Sheen's drama *The Temptress*, and also sustained a leading part in a piece, called *Under the Red Cross*, written by G. P. Nicholls, the Somersetshire cricketer, and dealing with incidents in the Boer War. He also acted with Mr Hill Mitchelson's company in a play called *Revenge*.

In 1887, while playing at theatres in and around Manchester, Atherston met a girl named Monica Kelly, the daughter of a law clerk. Before long, their friendship developed into romance, and in the late summer of 1888 (just when, incidentally, Jack the Ripper was getting into his stride) the couple were wed at a registry office in Monica's native borough of Salford, adjacent to Manchester. Monica's mother had been dead for some years, and her father had died shortly before the marriage, leaving her, an only child, all his worldly goods, which included a semi-detached house.

Thomas moved in with Monica. His frequent absences on tour seem to have made their respective hearts grow fonder, and during the first half-dozen years of the marriage, Monica gave birth to four children, two of whom were boys.

But in the final winter of the century, Thomas joined a company that numbered among its members a twenty-five-year-old actress called Elizabeth Earle. He fell in love with her. And she with him.

1. A tragedy by Nicholas Rowe, first produced in London, at Drury Lane, in 1714.

If pictures of Elizabeth treat her fairly, it is not unkind to say that she was plain: she had too much forehead, small lips that tended to purse, and tired-looking grey eyes. Still, one should not judge a book by its cover – Elizabeth must have possessed qualities that no camera or artist detected, for the tall, dark and handsome Thomas fell for her to such an extent that, at the end of the tour, he returned to Salford only from a sense of politeness, to inform Monica that he was leaving her and the children for another woman. He would have liked a divorce, but Monica, a devout Catholic, wouldn't hear of it.

Thomas travelled to London, where Elizabeth was awaiting him. Once again, he was residentially lucky, because Elizabeth lived with her elderly and ailing mother in a three-bedroom flat near Battersea Park, just south of the Thames, and he was allotted the spare bedroom. As soon as Mrs Earle died, *two* of the bedrooms became spare. We know this from Elizabeth herself, who some years later confessed that she and Thomas had 'an extremely intimate relationship'.

When he had theatrical engagements, they saw little of each other except from late at night until early in the morning. Elizabeth had given up performing to become a teacher at the Academy of Dramatic Art (which subsequently earned Royal approval, and is best known nowadays simply as RADA), and by the time she returned to the flat, Thomas had left, or was preparing to leave, for the first-house performance at whatever suburban theatre he was playing at; on Saturdays and Sundays, she eked out her earnings by giving tuition to private pupils.

From about the time that Thomas accepted the 'blackleg job' at the Bedford, when he was experiencing increasing difficulty in getting work and was stuck at home for weeks on end, he began to behave, as Elizabeth thought, 'peculiarly' and to seek excuses for arguing.

The die was cast. Directly or indirectly, Thomas Weldon Atherston's changed behaviour would result in murder.

Towards the end of 1909, he moved out of the first-floor flat in Prince of Wales Road, where he had been living with Elizabeth for some ten years, ever since he had deserted his wife and children. The reason for the break-up seems clear – his despondency during long periods of unemployment had caused him to fall out with Elizabeth, then to accuse her of having affairs with other men (entirely without foundation, according to her) – but there is no indication whether she, at the end of her tether, sent him packing or he left of his own volition.

If the latter explanation is right, he might have thought twice about forsaking Elizabeth had he not known that he could move into similarly cheap, though less comfortable, London digs. During most of his adult life, he had been fortunate in having few household expenses: first, his wife had inherited her father's house in Salford, then he had lived virtually rent-free with Elizabeth. And now he could take advantage of the fact that his two sons had come to London and were sharing a flat in Great Percy Street, near King's Cross railway station. He beseeched them to let bygones be bygones about his shabby treatment of their mother – and, indeed, of them and their sisters – and they agreed to make room for him.

Both sons had clerical jobs in the City. The elder, Frederick, who was in his early twenties, bore some physical resemblance to his father, being tall and lean, with an aquiline nose and dark hair that he made to shine almost dazzlingly through the application of pomade; though he had no special interest in the theatre, it may be that he had inherited some of his father's acting talent. William, Frederick's junior by about a year, also was dark, but noticeably shorter. Of course, though their father was known as Atherston, the sons had retained the family name of Anderson.

They had met Elizabeth Earle soon after their arrival in London. One surmises that before that first meeting, they had thought of her as a scarlet woman, the *femme fatale* who had lured Thomas from their mother; but they both got to like her.

Frederick especially was fond of Elizabeth, and when she and his father gave up living together, he became a frequent visitor at her flat. Later, William Anderson would be asked if he knew why his brother saw so much of Elizabeth, and would reply, rather unhelpfully, 'No ... except that he was on very good terms with her.' That, so far as I can tell, is the most that was ever said publicly about Frederick's relations with the thirty-five-year-old tutor of dramatic skills.

The break between Thomas and Elizabeth was not complete. When he left to live with his sons, he did not hand over the key to her flat; and presumably he used it at least once, in the middle of May 1910, when he called upon her and stayed the night. According to Elizabeth, 'He seemed sulky, and at breakfast next morning we quarrelled because he said I had had another man in the flat. He pointed to the sofa and said that it was indented and had been lain on. He struck me, and I called for help. Then I went into Battersea Park. On my return, he said, "It's all over." Before he went, he left the latch-key.'

But he returned on the following Saturday afternoon. If he hoped to find her alone so that he could attempt reconciliation, he was disappointed, for she was entertaining his son Frederick. After she had served tea, he left.

Perhaps on that occasion he was comparatively cheerful. He had at last obtained an engagement, a short tour in a play by a man called Fred Moule, who had put up the money for the production. Mr Moule afterwards said, 'Starting on Monday, 30 May, at Bow

Palace, he played for me at Sadler's Wells, then weeks at the Foresters, the Battersea Palace and the Surrey Theatre, finishing on Saturday, 2 July.[1] He was jealous – of whom, or on account of whom, he did not say. He added that he felt very keenly the parting with a charming lady in whose flat he had lodged for many years. He spoke of her as an intellectual companion, one who sympathized with him in his love of books and could talk to him. He mentioned no one by name, but he was clearly very upset about the breaking of the friendship. While we were at the Battersea Palace I said, "It's a pity you don't live in Prince of Wales Road, since you would not have so far to go home." He replied: "It's finished. That home will never be open to me again."'

On the second Wednesday after the suburban tour, Thomas stayed out all night. It appears that, when he turned up next day, neither of his sons inquired where he had been. Frederick casually mentioned that he was planning to visit Elizabeth on the following Saturday evening, and Thomas remarked, seemingly with equal casualness, 'Very likely I'll be there, too.'

For an account of what happened round about half-past nine on that Saturday evening, one is reliant on what was afterwards said by Elizabeth and Frederick.

She had recently had her bedroom redecorated, and, just before serving supper, she showed Frederick the result. They ate in the large kitchen at the rear of the

1. The Bow Palace was in Bow Road, East London; Sadlers Wells was – and, reconstructed, is – in Rosebery Avenue, Finsbury, EC1; the Foresters Music Hall was in Cambridge Heath Road, Bethnal Green – half a mile or so east of the Bow Palace; the Battersea Palace was in York Road, the continuation, to the south-west, of Battersea Park Road, which runs directly south of and roughly parallel with Prince of Wales Drive (which, in 1910, was called Prince of Wales Road); the Surrey Theatre was at the southern tip of Blackfriars Road, Lambeth, SE1.

flat. But they had barely begun when they were startled by two loud explosions.

Unmistakably gunfire. Less surely, from the direction of the back yard.

Although the terrace of red-brick houses was called Clifton Gardens, the yards were small, each made L-shaped by the abutment of the kitchens. The back doors of the two upstairs flats led on to the platforms of an iron fire-escape that descended in the crook formed by the meeting of the side wall of the kitchens with each of the main buildings.

Elizabeth followed Frederick as he opened the back door and stood on the platform. The flat was in the second house of the terrace, the corner house being a preparatory school, uninhabited at weekends. Looking to their right, they saw the figure of a person crouching on top of the high, ivy-covered wall that separated the yard of the school from the side-street. Elizabeth pulled Frederick back into the kitchen and locked the door. When they stared through the window, the person had disappeared from the top of the wall.

With remarkable composure, it might be thought, they resumed their supper. But after five minutes or so, they were again interrupted, this time by a knock at the front door. Frederick, very much at home, went to answer it, and found a policeman on the landing. The constable's name was David Buckley (which makes a small coincidence: nine months before, when the Stalybridge tycoon, George Harry Storrs, had been fatally stabbed at Gorse Hall, his mansion overlooking the cotton-town, the first policeman on the scene was a constable called David Buckley). After explaining that he was 'investigating an intimation from a member of the public that gun-shots had been fired in the vicinity', Buckley asked if he could go down the fire-escape to examine the yard; he mentioned that he had noticed that the ground-floor flat was empty, with a 'to let' sign on the window.

While Elizabeth waited on the platform of the fire-escape, Frederick followed Buckley down the steps. They looked around the yard, and at first observed nothing unusual. Then Frederick heard a faint sound: not unlike the whimpering of a neglected dog. The sound came from beneath the fire-escape.

A man was lying there, his head towards the kitchen door of the ground-floor flat, which was standing ajar. Buckley called out to Elizabeth to fetch a lamp. She did so, and Buckley asked Frederick to hold the lamp close to the body.

Kneeling, Buckley saw that the man was alive, but only just. A bullet had entered the left temple and come out through the right eye-socket; there was another bullet-wound in the right cheek, close to the mouth.

'Have you ever seen this man before?' the constable asked Frederick.

'No, I don't know anything about him,' was the reply.

Considering the identity of the dying man, Frederick's answer was most odd.

By the time that Detective-Inspector Emanuel Geake arrived at Clifton Gardens, the man found in the back yard had died. Frederick had returned to the first-floor flat.

Before perusing the contents of the dead man's pockets, Geake was caused to hesitate, perhaps scratching his head the while, by his observation of the dead man's footwear: though otherwise dressed for the street, he was wearing, not boots, but a pair of carpet-slippers, the tops fashioned from felt that had been dyed with red, purple and blue to make a fleur-de-lys pattern. Rummaging in the pockets, Geake found a gold watch (sans chain), 2/11d in coins, a memorandum book, and an elastic-banded pack of visiting-cards printed with the words,

T. Weldon Atherston
Leading Character Actor
7 Great Percy Street, London, W.C.

But Geake's most surprising find came from the back trouser-pocket: a home-made 'life-preserver', concocted from an eighteen-inch-long piece of heavy electric cable bound with string, one end of which was knotted into a loop to fit over the wrist – the whole thing making a very dangerous weapon indeed.

Trying to forge some sort of unity from what he had so far seen – the carpet-slippers, the visiting-cards of an actor, the life-preserver – Greake wandered into the ground-floor flat. There were plenty of signs that the place was being redecorated, and the inspector noted that the workmen had fixed a length of cord so that the lock on the front-door could be opened from the outside, making it easy for themselves – and anyone else – to enter.

On the kitchen mantelpiece, neatly wrapped in brown paper, was a pair of boots. Geake checked their size with that of the carpet-slippers. There was a matching. It was a mind-swaying thought, but apparently the man now lying dead in the yard had come into the flat, changed his boots for slippers that he had brought with him, and then, obsessively tidy, made a parcel of his boots and placed it on the shelf.

The inspector climbed the fire-escape to Elizabeth Earle's flat. Speaking to Frederick Anderson, he said, 'You told Constable Buckley that you don't know the dead man?'

'That's right,' Frederick replied. 'I know nothing about him.'

'Do you know anyone named Atherton?' (Geake, who had only glanced at the visiting-cards, had made a slight mistake in the name.)

'No,' Frederick said. A moment later, however, he volunteered the information: 'I know someone called Atherston.'

Geake placed one of the cards on the table, and at once Frederick said, 'That is my father's card.'

Elizabeth, the ex-actress, began to weep. The inspector escorted her into the freshly-wallpapered bedroom, then returned and informed Frederick: 'You'll have to come with me to the station.'

For the first time, it seems, the young man looked truly concerned. 'I can't do that,' he said. 'I haven't a latch-key, and if I don't get into my lodgings by half-past eleven, I'll be locked out.

Geake felt that, in view of the circumstances, that was an insufficient excuse. He insisted that Frederick accompany him to the station.

There, he showed Frederick the boots, and asked if he recognized them.

'Yes,' was the reply, 'they are my father's.' Then, at long last, he was struck by a thought similar to that which, back at the flat, had induced Elizabeth to weep. 'Good God,' he exclaimed, 'do you mean that it was my father who was shot? – my father whom I found lying there?'

The inspector's response was terse. 'It's no use asking me,' he snapped. 'You were there. I was not.'

'But that man didn't look like my father. Unless – was he wearing a false moustache?'

Geake shook his head. Perhaps he was thinking that the dead man's son might, just might, have mistaken the bullet-wound close to the mouth for a lop-sided moustache.

An hour or so later, at the mortuary, the body was definitely identified as that of Thomas Weldon Atherston. By then, the memorandum book found in one of the pockets had been scrutinized. Several entries indicated that ever since the actor had left or been thrown out by his mistress, he had spied on her movements, and one of the last notes read, 'If he had kept away from her, this would never have happened. He has no one to thank but himself.' There was no clue to who 'he' was.

Next day, Emanuel Geake interviewed three persons who claimed to have seen a man running either from

Clifton Gardens or from that direction. Though the night had been dark, all three felt able to give some description of him. The consensus of their recollections was that he was young, clean-shaven, of medium height, and smartly dressed.

The references to the man's sartorial elegance were of special interest to Geake.

He could be sure of only a few very basic things that had happened at about 9.30 on the Saturday night, but it was possible that Atherston, intensely jealous of Elizabeth Earle, had gone to Clifton Gardens to spy on her. Perhaps he had changed into his slippers, not for cosiness, but so as to proceed stealthily up the fire-escape, from the first platform of which he could peer into Elizabeth's kitchen. Had Atherston's plan gone awry because, by a shocking coincidence, just after he had put on the slippers and made the neat parcel of his boots, a burglar had entered the empty ground-floor flat? If that was what had happened – and if the burglar was carrying a pistol – then the murder was explained.

But Geake could not accept that theory. For one thing, the only burglar he had heard of who wore his Sunday-best at work was the fictional Raffles. For another, *armed* burglars almost invariably went for rich pickings, and there was nothing of much value in either Elizabeth Earle's flat or the one above (which was, by the way, empty at the time, the tenant being on holiday at Bognor Regis).

Whether he knew it or not, Emanuel Geake followed a dictum propounded by Sherlock Holmes: When you have eliminated the impossible – in this instance, the notion of a murderous burglar – whatever is left, however improbable, must be the truth. The improbable residue of his process of elimination was the brief that he was dealing with a case of patricide:

The actor's sons, with Elizabeth Earle an accessory, had committed the murder.

One had to look into Geake's mind, for he was never

able to voice his belief in public. There were at least three possible motives for the crime. If Frederick and his father's erstwhile mistress had fallen in love, then Thomas Weldon Atherston, jealously spying on Elizabeth, and quite prepared to use his home-made life-preserver, had to be eliminated; Frederick and his younger brother William, who were devoted to each other – and to their mother, who had been deserted by Atherston, leaving her to bring up four small children – may have decided that the ultimate revenge would be sweet; or they may simply have chosen to rid themselves of Atherston rather than face the prospect of having him living with them, sponging from them, until he died a natural death.

If it was William Anderson who was seen running away, then Frederick's slowness in 'recognizing' the victim as his father is understandable. William – carrying the gun, though it may have been Frederick who had fired it – needed time to get away, to hide the weapon, to clean himself up, to cool himself down. Frederick provided the time by delaying identification.

Were the brothers, with Elizabeth Earle, conspirators in a murder plot? One cannot say for sure. Inspector Geake sought evidence against them, but the case remained officially unsolved. Elizabeth moved from Clifton Gardens soon after the murder, and no more is heard of the brothers. Perhaps the three of them came together at some secluded rendezvous, there to congratulate one another on a job well done and to drink a toast: 'Good riddance to Thomas Weldon Atherston – a rotten parent, an unsuccessful actor, a lover who became expendable.' I wish I could make up my mind whether I hope that they lived happily ever after.

The Fate of the Fat Man

The names of celebrities, past or present, summon up different associations for different people. Mention the names of Roscoe Arbuckle and Mabel Normand to a solemn-minded film-fan, and he will probably reel off the titles of all the one- and two-reel silent comedies featuring 'Fatty and Mabel'. But to someone with a vicarious interest in crime, a reference to Mabel Normand may jog memories of the killing of William Desmond Taylor, while Roscoe 'Fatty' Arbuckle will be recalled as the defendant in another murder case of the same period.

By the late summer of 1921, Arbuckle, the son of a poor Kansas farmer, had risen from the ranks of the Keystone Kops to become a star, second only to Charlie Chaplin as a box-office attraction. Rotund enough to be jokingly called an 'all-round entertainer', he was entitled to the description as it is usually applied. Though only thirty-four, he had been in or on the periphery of show business for nearly a quarter of a century; prior to his arrival in Hollywood, he had been a song-and-dance man, a female inpersonator, a musical-comedy actor, and a contestant – often victorious – in pie-ingesting competitions.

It was as a *chucker* of pies, customarily the custard-capped kind, that he made his name in films: according to a columnist who believed that nothing succeeds like excess, Arbuckle's marksmanship and sense of timing made him

> the supreme grand lama of the meringue, the Hercules of the winged dessert, the Ajax of the hurtling fritter, the paragon of patty-casters, the unconquerable and valiant flinger of open and

closed mince models, the monarch of the zoom-
ing rissole.

Arbuckle had recently signed a contract that would
earn him close to three thousand dollars a day. A vast
amount – but he was worth every cent of it, the studio
bosses believed. After all, not only was he extremely
popular with the public but he was the most hard-
working and reliable star in Hollywood. Having made
half a dozen full-length films, including the smash-hit
Brewster's Millions, in the first seven months of 1921,
he had agreed to work on three feature films *simulta-
neously* during August, dashing from one set to
another, changing costume, playing a scene, then
rushing to the next set that had been erected in the
meantime. (One is reminded of the story of the actor in
a different-play-each-performance repertory company,
who, drying up, whispered to the prompter, 'What's
the line?' only to hear the whispered response, 'What's
the play?')

As it turned out, none of the three films was ever
released. There is a certain irony in the fact that, if the
films had been made consecutively, Arbuckle, the
'workaholic', would not have taken a break – would
not, in the company of a couple of friends, have driven
the 500 miles to San Francisco in his Pierce-Arrow
automobile (which numbered among its extra fittings a
drinks cabinet and a privy) for the long Labour-Day
weekend – would not have had his career ruined.

Arbuckle and his friends – a movie director named
Fred Fischbach and the actor Lowell Sherman –
reached San Francisco in the late afternoon of Saturday, 3 September. Having parked in the garage of the St
Francis, the grandest hotel in the city, they were taken
up in an elevator to an L-shaped suite, two bedrooms
separated by a parlour, that had been reserved for
them. By all accounts, they had an early night.

Next morning, ignoring the 'noble experiment' of

the Volstead Act, which was intended to prohibit the
sale and consumption of liquor, Arbuckle arranged for
crates of whisky and gin to be delivered to the suite. In
the afternoon, he had at least one visitor: a girl called
Mae Taube, who called at the suggestion of his friend,
the actress Bebe Daniels. Arbuckle and his companions
spent the evening at a club.

Some time during that evening, three other people
arrived in San Francisco from Hollywood. The trio
was composed of a twenty-five-year-old film actress,
Virginia Rappe, her agent Al Semnacher, and an
acquaintance of his, Maude 'Bambina' Delmont.

Virginia Rappe (who was careful to pronounce her
name 'Rap-*pay*') was a brunette, five feet seven inches
tall, and not particularly petite: she weighed just over 9½
stone. She had been trying to 'make it' in Hollywood
for five years, but without success. Her one claim to
fame was that, as a teenage model, she had been
pictured on the sheet-music for the song, 'Let Me Call
You Sweetheart'.

Following her death, tabloid newspapers sought to
explain how she could have survived in Hollywood for
so long with so little work: she designed dresses, said
one; she was the love-child of an English nobleman
who had spent some time in the States, claimed
another; she was a woman 'of independent wealth as a
result of oil investments', ventured a third. In the
opinion of Buster Keaton – admittedly, a friend of
Roscoe Arbuckle's – 'she was about as virtuous as most
of the other untalented young women who had been
knocking around Hollywood for years, picking up
small parts any way they could'.

But I have run slightly ahead of the story. In the late
morning of the Monday, Labour Day, someone or
other in Arbuckle's party, perhaps Roscoe himself,
somehow or other learned that Virginia Rappe was
staying at the Palace Hotel, and asked her round to the
suite at the St Francis. She accepted the invitation, and

turned up at noon, accompanied by Al Semnacher and Maude Delmont.

The suite was already crowded, and it became more so as time went by. Illicit booze was guzzled (though not by Virginia, who, so it is said, sipped just three 'orange-blossoms', a concoction of gin and orange juice); some of the girls permitted petting, others encourage cuddling; couples jigged to ragtime music from the Victrola.

There are conflicting stories of what happened in the middle of the afternoon, close to three o'clock. The only important thing one can be sure of is that Virginia Rappe suddenly experienced excruciating pains in her lower abdomen and let out a number of screams.

A doctor who was called made a perfunctory examination, asked a few questions of Arbuckle and some of the guests, and concluded that Virginia was suffering from an extravagance of bootleg gin. Eventually, the girl was taken to an empty room in the hotel. Other doctors who saw her seem to have taken a 'time-is-the-great-healer' attitude to her condition. But as she was still suffering on Thursday, she was removed to a sanatorium. She died there on Friday afternoon, four days after the party.

An autopsy showed that Virginia Rappe's bladder was ruptured: death was ascribed to peritonitis.

On the basis of allegations made by Maude 'Bambina' Delmont, Roscoe 'Fatty' Arbuckle was charged under the section of the penal code that provided that 'a life taken in rape or attempted rape is considered *murder*'.

ACTRESS DIES AFTER HOTEL PARTY

FATTY ARBUCKLE SOUGHT IN ORGY DEATH

Headlines like those, splashed across the front pages of newspapers, English as well as American, had an

instant extra-legal effect: distributors and exhibitors of
Roscoe Arbuckle's films, advertised as being 'Fun for
All the Family', decided that discretion was the better
part of staying in business; many cinemas changed
programmes in mid-week, and some of those and
others stripped posters for 'Arbuckle Romps' from the
forthcoming-attraction boards. One moment, Arbuckle was the chubby-cheeked clown with a bemused
smile and an unerring aim with custard-pies – the next,
he was an obese rapist who had caused the death of a
poor frightened young girl, appropriately named Virginia, who was only half his size.

The actions of the distributors and exhibitors were
belated compared with those taken by the bosses of
Arbuckle's studio. Some time before it was generally
known that Virginia Rappe was dead, the bosses
attempted a cover-up – tried to protect the reputation
of their hottest property. Money was offered to, and
accepted by, staff at the sanatorium where the girl had
died. How else can one explain the fact that, only an
hour or so after the death, an autopsy was carried out
in secret and the remains then despatched to an
undertaker? The autopsy was illegal, since permission
for it had not been obtained from a coroner.

Only by chance did a coroner learn of the unusual
death – of the secret probing of the body. He told the
press. Reporters looked into the circumstances leading
to Virginia Rappe's death, learned of the Labour-Day
party at the St Francis Hotel, listened to Maude
Delmont's account of how the girl had been 'outraged'
by Arbuckle.

Miss (or maybe Mrs) Delmont's story was very
different from the one told by Arbuckle. According to
him:

> At my invitation, [Virginia Rappe and her two
> friends] came to my rooms to have a few drinks. I
> was clad in pyjamas, bathrobe and bedroom

slippers .... Shortly after Miss Rappe had taken a few drinks, she became hysterical, complained that she could not breathe, and then started to tear off her clothes. I requested two girls present at the time to take care of Miss Rappe. She was disrobed and placed in a bath-tub to be revived. The immersion did not benefit her, and I then telephoned to the hotel manager, telling him what was wrong, and requested that Miss Rappe be given a room. She was taken out of my room and put to bed.

When no change came in Miss Rappe's condition, I summoned a physician. I departed from the St Francis Tuesday ....

I was at no time alone with Miss Rappe. During the time in my rooms, there were at least half a dozen people there all the time, and I can produce witnesses to bear out that statement. I am only too glad to return to San Francisco from Hollywood to assist the authorities in straightening out this horrible mess.

The 'horrible mess' was partly caused by suspicions raised by the secret autopsy. Only partly. The main cause was Maude Delmont's version of what had happened in the hotel suite between about two and three o'clock on the hot Monday afternoon.

She said that she was standing with other guests, admiring the view from a window in the parlour, when Virginia sidled up to her and whispered that Roscoe Arbuckle had 'got hold of her' in the bathroom adjoining his bedroom. A few minutes later, Maude noticed that Virginia had returned to the bathroom with Arbuckle. Then she saw Arbuckle emerge from the bathroom, walk across the bedroom, and close the door. Taking a live-and-let-live attitude to what she surmised was going on behind the door, Maude joined Arbuckle's actor-friend Lowell Sherman, and they danced – energetically, it seems, for after a while she told Sherman that she would feel more comfortable if she were to remove her clothes and slip into pyjamas. He took her into the other bedroom, lent her a pair of buttercup-coloured silk pyjamas, and, the perfect gentleman, left her alone while she changed. Then they continued dancing.

About half an hour later, Maude wondered about Virginia and Arbuckle, who were still in the latter's bedroom. She knocked on the door, called out to Virginia, then tried to open the door. It was locked. She took off a shoe and knocked on the door with the heel. Still no response. None of the revellers paid any attention. She looked around for Virginia's agent Al Semnacher, but there was no sign of him. She banged on the door again. No one answered.

But then came the sound of piercing screams from the bedroom. After repeatedly banging on the door, Maude telephoned to the hotel desk. An assistant manager arrived, and at that moment the bedroom door opened and Arbuckle appeared, his pyjamas wringing wet. Virginia's panama hat was perched on his head, and he was smiling – 'his foolish screen smile', to use Maude's words.

Guests rushed into the bedroom. Virginia was lying on the larger of the two beds; she was screaming and pulling at her clothes. She started to tear the clothes from her body, and as she did so, she shrieked:

'I am hurt. I am dying. He did it, Maudie.'

She was still screaming and now clutching her stomach as some of the guests carried her into the bathroom and deposited her in the tub, already filled with cold water. When she had been towelled down, Roscoe and the assistant manager carried her to an empty room along the corridor.

That was Maude Delmont's account. And it was her version rather than Arbuckle's that Matthew Brady, the district attorney of San Francisco, chose to believe.

A week after the party, and three days after the death of Virginia Rappe, the DA accompanied Maude to a courthouse, where she swore out a murder complaint against Roscoe Arbuckle.

It never occurred to anyone that she would *not* be the star prosecution witness when Arbuckle stood trial for his life. But by the time the case came to court, the district attorney had discovered that Maude Delmont was an unconvicted bigamist, a fact that could be used by defence counsel to discredit her as a witness. Bending the legal process, Brady delayed charging her with bigamy – but, just to be on the safe side, as the defence might have learned her guilty secret, did not call her as a witness against Arbuckle. This meant that the prosecution case was like a custard-pie without custard: the central, salient, testimony was missing.

Making the best of a thoroughly bad job, Brady persuaded lesser witnesses to 'improve' their evidence and caused witnesses who might have helped the defence to be hidden away. Entering into the spirit of things, the defence engaged in similar shenanigans.

Unsurprisingly, considering the gaps in the evidence on both sides and the obvious lies told by several witnesses, the jury were unable to reach a verdict. A second trial also resulted in a 'hung jury' (as at the first, there was a majority of 10–2 in Arbuckle's favour). At the third trial, the jury took only five minutes to decide on acquittal. When the verdict had been announced, the foreman read out a statement that sounded suspiciously like a press agent's hand-out:

> Acquittal is not enough for Roscoe Arbuckle. We feel that a great injustice has been done him. We feel also that it was only our plain duty to give him this exoneration, under the evidence, for there was not the slightest proof adduced to connect him in any way with the commission of a crime .... The happening at the hotel was an

unfortunate affair for which Arbuckle, so the evidence shows, was in no way responsible. We wish him success ....

That wish did not come true. Many people questioned the verdict; for others, the long-drawn-out legal proceedings and the publicity attendant on them had irreparably tarnished Arbuckle's image. And, to make matters worse for him, the Hollywood moguls had reacted to the affair by appointing William Hays, a Presbyterian politician, as watchdog over films and film-makers: in so doing, they had condemned Arbuckle, if not as a rapist and murderer, at least as a person who had given the whole industry a bad name.

Over the next decade, he appeared in night-clubs, went on a short-lived tour of vaudeville theatres, and, using the alias of William Goodrich (as opposed to 'Will B. Good', the name suggested by wags), directed a few films.

In 1933, Warner Brothers engaged him to appear in a series of two-reelers. Pleased with the result, the company signed him up to star in a feature film. It seemed that he was about to make a come-back. But that same night, he died from a heart attack.

Some of the obituaries were generous, but one paper commented, 'We no longer speak of him', adding that, so far as the paper was concerned, his death had been announced shortly after the disastrous party at the St Francis Hotel, San Francisco.

The Paganini of Crime

So-called crime-waves, if they come to an end, usually dwindle towards that end; only rarely do they cease abruptly. But in the pitch-black early-morning hours of Thursday, 10 October 1878, a single arrest – made only after the criminal had fired five shots from a pistol, the last bullet striking a constable in the arm – brought to a sudden conclusion an epidemic of burglaries that had afflicted denizens of South-East London for eighteen months or so. It also, incidentally, permitted the constabulary of the steel city of Sheffield to close its file on a murder case, and led to the release from gaol of a young Irishman wrongly convicted of another murder, that of a policeman at Whalley Range, near Manchester.

The news of the arrest of Mr John Thompson, and the subsequent reports of the activities that had made him a singular crime-wave, caused much surprise among the residents of Evelina Road, a quiet thoroughfare of substantial villas in the district of London, south of the Thames, called Peckham. Admittedly, their ex-neighbour had *looked* a trifle unbecoming, what with his monkey-like, seamed features, his cinnamon skin, made to appear darker by the lint-white of his hair, his diminutiveness, and that peculiar gait of his, as if he were on tiptoe. And, yes, it *struck* them as strange that the Thompsons employed no domestic servants, and that such a well-to-do couple needed to share their eight-roomed domicile with lodgers, a drab creature called Hannah and her taciturn son, Willie.

But, the aforementioned oddities apart, Mr Thompson had given the impression of being a cultivated old gentleman; indeed, his presence had added a touch of 'tone' to Evelina Road. How? Well, take, for instance, the regular musical *soirées* No. 5, when Mr Thompson had treated the guests to renditions of popular classics on the violin, his spouse accompanying him on the pianoforte, young Willie occasionally adding to the artistic din by strumming his Spanish guitar – or whatever that instrument-thing of his was. A versatile entertainer, Mr Thompson had often followed his violin recital with a few recitations from the polite poets – or a single lone one: 'The Dream of Eugene Aram', perhaps – and then finished off the evening, an uplifting time having been had by all, by warbling some Moody & Sankey hymns or ballads of a sentimental and/or inspiring nature, encouraging audience participation the while.

Not wishing to pry, the neighbours had been unable to ascertain how Mr Thompson, who followed no regular daytime occupation, was able to live in such fine style – immaculately-polished walnut furniture, glistening silver, sparkling crystal, and all that; there was surmise that one of the sundry inventions he spoke about, perhaps the scheme he had been discussing with a local gentleman to raise sunken ships by pumping air into the holds, had been acquired by a large company, even by Her Majesty's government, and brought in substantial royalties.

None of the respectable residents of Evelina Road, not one of them, had ever doubted the respectability of Mr John Thompson. No wonder, then, that they got the shock of their lives when the arrested Mr Thompson was revealed to be not a novice sinner but an 'arch criminal', and that their surprise knew no bounds when he was described, without hyperbole, as probably the most industrious, ingenious and ruthless villain of all time. Why, even the name they knew him by was bogus. His real name, which could hardly have been more inapt, was *Peace*.

Not only was Peace's name inapt, but, rather like his dualism, his place of birth was heavenly-sounding but sordid. Angel Court, it was called. The court, actually a blind-alley, was even more of a slum than the Sheffield slums that surrounded it.

Charles Peace was born there on 14 May 1832. His parents, who already had three children, two boys and a girl, would never have been brought together by any of those present-day computerized dating services that 'think' in terms of the attraction of similarities. John Peace, a man in his forties, had only one leg; he had lost the other in a coal-mining accident when he was young, and had then become, it is safe to say, the only one-legged lion-tamer in the country, touring the counties of the White Rose and the Red with a circus, before settling in Sheffield, where, unprosperously, he ran a shoemaking shop. His wife, who was nearly a score of years his junior, was the daughter of a naval surgeon.

In 1844 – by which time the family was better off, for John Peace had changed occupations yet again, now being a coal-merchant (though he was toying with the idea of giving *that* up and taking over a pub) – Charles left school and, after a brief apprenticeship to a tinsmith, worked in a steel mill.

Not for long, however. While he was helping a boy operating the machine next to his, a shaft of red-hot steel rolled through his own machine and pierced his left leg, entering the thigh on one side and emerging just below the knee on the other. After the roller had been reversed to pull out the length of steel, he was carried to a hospital, where his kneecap was removed. Though the severity of the injury kept him in hospital for a year and a half, he was more fortunate than his father: he did not lose the limb. Soon discarding his crutches, he not only tried to disguise the infirmity in one leg by adopting a tiptoeing gait with both, but taught himself acrobatics and developed a tumbling act which he performed in the pubs and gin-palaces of the city.

To augment the act, and thus to increase the 'nobbings' thrown to him by spectators, he learnt the violin from an itinerant musician named Joe Bethley, known to cronies as Manger, who around about this time took Charles's sister into his lodgings, where, among other activities, she bore him three children, none of whom was given a semblance of legitimacy.

Charles developed a certain skill as a violinist – though not such as to justify his billing himself as 'The Modern Paganini' when he tried to break into the professional theatre. David Ward[1] found out that

> he joined a society of amateurs who formed themselves into a concert party .... These keen young men dreamt of success as professionals. They rented a disused theatre at Worksop and staged their first 'pro' venture. It was a terrible fiasco. On the second night a party of rowdies pelted them with rotten fruit and broke up the show for ever. The company had some difficulty raising their return fares to Sheffield.
>
> Theatricals had taught Peace some useful lessons. He had worked up an act in which he billed himself as 'The Great Ethiopian'. One evening, walking home after a concert, but without bothering to wash off the make-up he had used on his face on the stage, he met several acquaintances as he passed down the street where he lived .... It was not lost on him that they failed to recognize him beneath his dark mask. He had learned that in disguise he might well go undetected even by familiars.

The pliability of his body, together with the fact that

---

1. *King of the Lags*, published by Elek Books of London and the Ryerson Press of Toronto in 1963.

he was short and slim, proved advantageous when, having given up trying to break into the theatre, he tried to break into houses. Before then, however, his manual dexterity, perhaps enhanced by his fiddling, had made him a successful pickpocket: successful in the sense that he pilfered lots of trifling articles and small amounts of money without being caught.

He got off to a poor start as a burglar. At the age of nineteen, he and a much older accomplice escaped with diverse loot from the house of the mother of the Mayor of Sheffield; one of the stolen items (a pistol, the elderly woman's ownership of which does not seem to have perplexed anyone) was traced by the police to a pawn-shop, the pledge was proved to have been made by Charles, and, as there was insufficient evidence to sustain a charge of housebreaking, he was given a prison sentence of one month for receiving stolen goods.

After his release, undeterred by the short, sharp punishment, he took up housebreaking in earnest; but, his luck holding out, he was not arrested again until 1854, when, again through the evidence of a pawn broker, he was found guilty of a large number of robberies and was sent to prison for four years.

Caught trying to escape from Wakefield Gaol, he was lodged in the solitary-confinement block, where he attempted to commit suicide by hacking his throat with a nail. According to some writers, his experiences at Wakefield turned him into an 'enemy of society'. Well, perhaps: but I have discerned few signs that he was at all friendly towards society previously.

Anyway, he came out of prison in October 1858. If not at once, certainly soon after his release, he decided to try his villainous luck in Manchester.

There are several versions of how Charles Peace met Hannah Ward; since none of them can be confirmed, it is best to ignore all of them. Hannah, who was a widow with a baby called Willie when she first encountered Peace, is said to have married him in 1859; however, so far as I can make out, there is no documentary proof of this. Whether as husband and wife or without marital ties, the couple stuck together, though there were several gaps in the relationship, to the unnatural end of Peace's unnatural life.

Charles and Hannah were soon parted. In June 1859, he and a man named Alfred Newton, landlord of a pub in Sheffield, had a night out in Rusholme, near Manchester, for the purpose of burgling a mansion. Perhaps because they took such a large quantity of goods, too heavy to carry far, they stowed most of the loot in a sewer crossing a field at a place called Brightons Green, adjacent to Rusholme. Either the police were tipped off by an informer or the booty was found through serendipity, and when Charles and his publican crony returned to the field, they were surrounded by members of the local constabulary. There was a fierce fight, during which an officer was seriously hurt, before the thieves were manacled and dragged to the police station.

When charged, Peace gave his name as George Parker and said that he was a professor of music. At the subsequent trial at Manchester Assizes, he claimed an alibi for the night of the burglary. Despite the appearance of his mother in the witness-box, to support his alibi and to say what a good son he was, the jury found him guilty and he was sentenced to six years' penal servitude. Alfred Newton, who had not been caught burgling before, went to prison for a mere fifteen months.

By the time Peace was released, his daughter, Jane Ann, with whom Hannah had been overtly pregnant during the trial, was five years old. It may be that some paternal instinct persuaded Peace to try to 'go straight', with a picture-framing business in Sheffield. But he didn't try very hard.

The *Manchester Guardian* of 4 December 1866, reporting on the city's Winter Assizes, noted:

> George Parker, alias Alexander Mann, was indicted for burglary. The prosecutor, Mr W. R. Gemmell, lives in Victoria Park, Manchester. On the 29th of August he was disturbed about 4 a.m. by a noise and on his servants going downstairs they found the house had been entered through the kitchen window, that the dining room had been broken into, and that many things and some money had been stolen. The prisoner was apprehended a few minutes afterwards. He had in his possession property which was identified by the prosecutor, and a centre-bit, two gimblets, a punch, and other articles, In defence, Mr Torr simply raised the point that there was no proof that the house had been burglariously broken into.

Perhaps needless to say, George Parker, also known as Alexander Mann, was actually Charles Peace. And – again perhaps needless to say, considering the brevity of his defence – the report concluded:

> The jury found the prisoner guilty.

Peace prolonged the proceedings by making a rambling speech, in which he pleaded for mercy for his little daughter's sake and so on, but was told by the judge that the most mercy he could expect was a blind eye to the fact that he had burgled another house only an hour or so before he was caught in the one in Victoria Park. Peace's first prison sentence, when he was nineteen, had been for just a month, the second had been for four years, the third for six. This time, continuing the progression, he was sentenced to seven years' penal servitude.

Informed while he was in prison of the death of his son John, who had been conceived in the short time between the two Manchester sentences, Peace composed a poem to the boy he had never seen:

> Farewell, my dear son, by us all beloved,
> Thou are gone to dwell in the mansions above,
> In the bosum of Jesus who sits on the Throne,
> Thou are anxiously awaiting to welcome us home.

In August 1872, Peace was released on ticket-of-leave from what turned out to be his last long period in prison. He was now aged forty, but he looked a lot older, for his hair had turned nearly white. In the next few years, far from fretting about his senile appearance, he turned it to advantage – indeed, at times exaggerated his apparent age. It came in useful, for instance, when he was 'casing' a building: people were far less likely to be suspicious of an inquisitive old chap than of a spry young stranger. The white hair, the seamed features, and the shortness of stature added up to deception. Not only was Peace extremely agile and athletic, capable of scaling high walls, of squeezing through tiny openings, but he was a ferocious fighter, ready and willing to kick, gouge, bite, butt or punch his way out of trouble.

Soon after the start of his sentence for the robbery in Victoria Park, Hannah had opened a general shop in Long Millgate, Manchester; it is reasonable to assume that the starting capital was raised from the pawning of articles stolen by Charles and that some of the stock was ill-gotten. However, the retailing venture had foundered, and by the time Peace became a ticket-of-leave man, Hannah was back in Sheffield, living in the same mean street as the woman who may have been her mother-in-law, and eking out a meagre existence by doing odd jobs as a charwoman and as a washer of red-biddy bottles for a local wine merchant.

The reappearance of Charles heralded a period of prosperity for Hannah, young Willie, and the slightly younger Jane Ann, who had had a visible father for no more than about two of her thirteen years. Even now, though, Jane Ann usually only saw her dad during the day, when he was giving the appearance of earning his living from joinery, wood-carving and the framing of pictures. Most nights, he was skulking around one or another of the more desirable residential areas of the north of England, seeing what he could pick up. By 1875, some of what he had picked up during his travels had been converted into a nest-egg sufficient to warrant a move to a larger house in a rather better district of Sheffield.

Indirectly, the move would result in murder.

Peace didn't allow his affluence to show. The proceeds of his nocturnal activities were salted away, and so far as inquisitive persons – policemen, for instance – could see, his life-style matched the small income from his licit daytime trades. Hannah did her bit to support Charles's act: when they moved to Darnall, on the eastern side of Sheffield, she continued to wash bottles for the wine merchant near their previous home. And Willie contributed more to the keeping-down-with-the-Joneses deception than to the housekeeping kitty by running errands for a grocer.

The new address, doubly patriotic, was 40 Victoria Place, Britannia Road. A married couple named Dyson lived just two doors away in the terrace of bijou residences. Though their present existence was dull, Arthur and Catharine Dyson had known almost as much excitement as had their new neighbours; the big difference between the couples was that the Dysons could chat freely about their past.

As a young man, some thirty years before, Arthur had left Sheffield and emigrated to America, where, after adventures in the very wild west, he had become a railroad engineer, laying tracks across deserts and prairies and other flat stretches of land. He had met Catharine, a teenage Irish migrant, in Cleveland, Ohio, and after a brief courtship, married her. For the next ten years they had travelled the country, with Catharine cooking their meals and driving the buggy – sometimes, so she afterwards recalled, 'through forests where there were bears and over creeks swollen by floods, so that the horses had to swim'. Arthur's health had broken down while he was erecting a bridge over the Mississippi, and he, with Catharine, had returned to Sheffield, there to work in the office of a railway company.

The Dysons seemed an oddly-matched pair. Catharine, many years her husband's junior, pink-cheeked and raven-haired, was energetic and fun-loving; Arthur was lethargic, a lump of a man who, when he came home at night, had no wish to emerge.

But the contrast between the personalities of Mr and Mrs Dyson was no more extreme than the visual contrast between Arthur Dyson and Charles Peace, who introduced hinself as soon as the removal cart had trundled away and in no time was as often in the Dysons' house as he was in his own. Seen together, Dyson and Peace resembled, as an observer put it, 'an organ-grinder and his monkey', for Dyson – so tall that the railway company had needed to provide him with a bespoke desk - towered above Charles by some fifteen inches.

One gathers that, from the start, Dyson would have much preferred not to be seen with Peace; but he let politeness override his desire to be left alone Catharine, on the other hand, was intrigued by the little man. He was great fun, she thought. And she was flattered by his obvious infatuation with her. Whether, to use a euphemism of the time, she succumbed bodily to her gnome-like admirer is open to question; a year or so later, she expressed indignation at the very idea, but one cannot help wondering – and not because Peace, an enthusiastic liar, afterwards boasted that they had enjoyed each other's company, though none too comfortably, in the garret of the empty house that kept their homes apart.

There was nothing at all covert about Peace's infatuation. Soon the other dwellers in Victoria Place were gossiping about how he was always popping in to see Catharine Dyson while her husband was occupied at his outsize desk ... how he had been seen listening at the keyhole of the Dysons' front door ... how he had been seen peering through their windows. One wonders what Hannah thought of it all. And one wonders what was the last straw so far as Arthur Dyson was concerned.

Whatever it was, it provoked a most genteel reaction. Arthur wrote a message on one of his calling-cards – 'Charles Peace is requested not to interfere with my family' – and threw the card into his persecutor's front-garden.

Peace's response was far from genteel. He trailed the disconsolate Arthur through the streets, screaming threats and curses at him. And when Catharine broke off from an alfresco conversation with some neighbours to call out to him that he must stop annoying her husband, he produced a pistol, aimed it at her head, and snarled: 'I'll blow your bloody brains out – and your bloody husband's, too.'

Hearing of this incident from one of the endangered neighbours, Arthur was apparently so shocked by the use of foul language in the presence of ladies that he took out a summons against Peace.

Realizing that, as a ticket-of-leave man, he could go back to gaol for a long stretch for carrying a firearm and using it intimidatingly, Peace did a midnight flit before the police arrived. Incidentally, for a few nights before his departure, vast quantities of food were taken in a flurry of burglaries of local grocery shops and warehouses. Peace was stocking up in preparation for the opening of a café in the Yorkshire port of Hull.

While Hannah ran the business, Charles went on his

travels. These took him to Manchester – always one of his favourite hunting-grounds, despite the fact that he had twice been arrested there.

Late on the rainy night of 1 August 1876, he was inspecting property in the suburb of Whalley Range. In addition to his housebreaking tools, some of them of his own invention, he was carrying a pistol.

A twenty-year-old probationary constable, Nicholas Cock, was on beat-duty in the district. He had had a pretty full day. That morning, he had appeared in court to give evidence against three Irish brothers, the Habrons, in a case of drunkenness; the brothers were very angry about the charge, and after the proceedings, one of them had threatened to shoot Cock. 'Threatened men live long,' Cock's superior, Superintendent Bent, had reassured him.

A church clock was chiming twelve as the young policeman reached the junction of Chorlton-cum-Hardy Road and Seymour Grove. There he met a colleague, James Beanland, who told him of a stranger prowling around nearby. While Cock waited outside the large house on the corner of Seymour Grove, Beanland entered the grounds. Finding nothing suspicious, he had just started to retrace his steps when there were two explosions from the direction of the road. Rushing out of the grounds, he found Cock lying against the wall, with blood rushing from a mortal wound near the heart.

The investigation of the murder was led by Superintendent Bent. Recalling his last conversation with Cock, he arrested the three Habron brothers, who laboured and lived at a nursery less than a quarter of a mile from the scene of the murder. Apart from the threat made against Cock, there was very little to connect the brothers with the crime. One of them was soon discharged. However, the others were tried at Manchester Assizes in November. The jury acquitted one of them – but, perhaps as much because of general anger at recent Sinn Fein atrocities as because of an obviously false alibi, eighteen-year-old William Hab ron was found guilty.

Charles Peace looked down from the public gallery as the black-capped judge pronounced the death sentence. Was he sad ... or relieved? One or other of those feelings, surely, for it was he who had killed Police Constable Cock.

The day after the trial, Peace killed again. This time, though, the crime was not a spur-of-the-moment action to prevent capture: it was long premeditated, the culmination of a scheme, the final touch to the persecution of Arthur Dyson and his wife Catharine, the woman Peace had once been crazily infatuated with.

After Peace had departed from his house in Sheffield so as to avoid being arrested on the summons taken out by the sorely-tried Arthur, the Dysons, far from being allowed to forget their ex-neighbour, had received many intimations that he intended to exact revenge.

There were, for instance, the letters, posted in Hanburg, that rambled from pleas for forgiveness to obscene abuse, from cajolery to threats. (Peace may have persuaded a seaman on a Hull-Hamburg steamer to post the letters from Germany; if he posted them himself, the riddle of how he disposed of so much swag that was never traced could be partly explained.) The Dysons – and the police – were aware that, though Peace was no longer living in Sheffield, he sometimes visited the city: despite his disguises, some of them feminine, he was recognized as he skulked the street at night. And the Dysons knew that they were being spied upon – not only occasionally by Peace but regularly by his daughter's boy-friend, a miner named William Bolsover.

It was probably Bolsover who informed Peace that the Dysons were moving from Victoria Place. Their new residence, on the far side of Sheffield, was one of seven houses called Banner Cross Terrace. The Banner Cross Hotel stood at one end of the terrace, and at the far end, next to a house that was used as a general shop by Mrs Mary Gregory, was the house that the Dysons had acquired.

Twilight was gathering when the removal cart arrived there on 19 October 1876. As the removal men started to hump furniture into the house, a tiny, wizen-faced man approached them. He asked when the Dysons were coming, and was told that they were travelling by train and would be along directly. He then went into the shop – not to buy anything but to tell Mrs Gregory that her impending neighbours were 'bad people'. Leaving the astonished shopkeeper, he went back to the house and, pushing past the removal men, walked inside to examine the layout and to peer through the rear window at the common yard that ran the length of the terrace.

It was then that the Dysons arrived. As they entered the house – a refuge, so they had thought – Charles Peace tiptoed towards them. He was grinning. 'I'm here to annoy you, wherever you go,' he said. The grin faded, and he snarled a string of obscenities. Then he walked out into the street. William Bolsover was waiting for him. The wretched Dysons watched from the front door as their tormentor and his spy disappeared into the shadows.

A month passed: exactly a month. Near the end of that time, Peace, having committed robberies throughout the north of England, decided that he had earned a couple of days' relaxation. He sat through the trial of the Habron brothers for the murder of P.C. Cock at Whalley Range.

By the early afternoon of the next day, he was back in Sheffield, entertaining the customers of a pub near Banner Cross with jigs played on a 'violin' he had contrived from a piece of string and a poker and stick provided by the landlord. He had had a lot to drink by the time he left.

He did not go to Banner Cross – not at once, that is. He turned up at a vicarage, and insisted on telling the bemused cleric that he should be 'on his guard' against some new parishioners, the Dysons. Leaving the vicarage at about a quarter to seven, he moved closer to Banner Cross. At times, he was furtive; at others, seemingly anxious to publicize his presence, his intention. Afterwards, people would recall being accosted by a strange little man; one of them would remember incoherent comments about a shooting.

Peace entered Mrs Gregory's shop. Though he left almost immediately, the woman was so frightened that she bolted the door. Every so often, she looked through her kitchen window, hoping to catch sight of one of the Dysons.

A light drizzle was falling when, at about eight o'clock, she heard footsteps from the common yard. Through the window, she saw Catharine Dyson. A moment later, there was a piercing scream.

As Arthur Dyson appeared at his back door, Mrs Gregory opened hers. 'Mr Dyson, go to your wife,' she shouted.

He did so.

Two shots rang out.

The excessively tall Arthur Dyson collapsed on the cobble-stones.

Charles Peace raced towards the only exit from the yard as Catharine knelt by her husband. She tried to stroke away the blood that coursed from his left temple; had to be pulled away by Mary Gregory, who gently told her that Arthur was dying.

Although the explosions had brought people running out of their houses, the only person to witness Peace's escape was a boy. He saw the tiny figure rush across the road from Banner Cross Terrace and vault over a wall into a field.

The police issued a description of Peace – noting, among other particulars, that he had lost a finger from his left hand (just how was never established). A large reward was offered for information leading to his discovery and conviction. The homes of relatives and acquaintances were searched, and some of them afterwards kept under observation. Railway stations were watched, roads out of the city cordonned, canal locks patrolled.

But Peace remained at large. There are lots of stories of how he evaded capture in Sheffield, Manchester, Hull – indeed, just about every town in the north. One or two of the tales seem to be based on at least a grain of truth, but none can be wholly extracted from the mythology that eventually mongrelized Charles Peace as part goblin, part latter-day Robin Hood, and part (a very small part, this) Satanic monster.

There is evidence, apparently reliable, that early in 1877 he was in Nottingham. Either then or a few months later – in the Spring, perhaps – he was dossing with a Mrs Adamson, who was suspected by the Nottingham police of earning far more as a fence of stolen property than as a landlady.

One afternoon, while Peace was buttering a crumpet in Mrs Adamson's parlour, a new resident introduced herself. Her name was Susan Bailey. Thirty-five years of age, and with a husband somewhere or other, she bore – so it seemed to Peace – a striking resemblance to Catharine Dyson. Instantly smitten, he determined to make Susan his travelling companion, his sleeping partner in crime. After a few more teatime tête-à-têtes, during which Susan learnt that he had a mother in Hull (actually, he was referring to Hannah Peace, who, if not his wife, had been pretending to that title for about eighteen years), he made a proposition and Susan accepted. Posing as Mr and Mrs John Thompson, they went on a crooks' tour, eventually drifting to London.

Finding rich pickings in the metropolis, Peace

decided to settle down in the suburb of Peckham. By now, he had committed so many crimes in so many places without being caught that he honestly believed that he never *would* be caught. In this he was mistaken.

Charles was faithful to Hannah in his fashion. As soon as he and Susan – 'Mr and Mrs Thompson' – had moved into the house in Evelina Road, he arranged for Hannah to move in, too. And – oh, all right, if she insisted – to bring Willie with her.

Though most visitors were given the impression of domestic bliss, one or other of the foursome were usually at loggerheads with one or more of the others. The long time Hannah had spent with Peace (and, for that matter, with*out* him, when he was in gaol or on the run) had made her sour and neurotic. And, not surprisingly, she didn't put herself out to be cordial to the new woman in Peace's life.

Susan had been partial to a drop of gin and a pinch of snuff before she had encountered Peace – but now, with plenty of money but also a lot of anxiety, both provided by Charles, she was virtually a chain-snuffer, getting through half an ounce a day, and was knocking back neat gin as if it were water. Peace did not object to the snuff-taking, but he was concerned lest the gallons of 'mother's ruin' fuddle Susan's brain and lubricate her tongue, causing her to babble about his past and present mischieves. And so he detailed Hannah and Willie (who was himself rather a trial, surly and lazy, displaying no interest in anything other than his Spanish guitar, and not much in that) to take turns at chaperoning the unsteady, untrustworthy Susan.

At times, especially when Peace was feeling a trifle tired after a late burgling night, he was less than placid: then he was liable to give a good hiding to Hannah for pouting, to Susan for having had one over the eighteen, and to Willie for doing nothing. When sorely tried, he would produce the pistol that he had used to murder

Nicholas Cock in Manchester and Arthur Dyson in Sheffield, and threaten to use it again, this time for a domestic murder in Peckham.

He was happiest when he was being inventive – either in company with his new-found friend, Henry Brion, who was full of good ideas (for raising sunken ships, for irrigating the Sahara, for walking through fire without getting one's eyebrows singed), or alone in his workshop, where he concocted tools and gadgets as addenda to his manual burgling skills.

Summer or winter, when he went out at night he was usually clad in an overcoat: Hannah, a good needle-woman, had sewn poacher's pockets inside the coat – useful, these, for both tools and loot. And sometimes he would carry a violin-case – containing, of course, burglarious devices of one sort or another.

But in the early hours of Thursday, 10 October 1878, he was empty-handed. At least, he *was* as he tiptoed through the ground-floor rooms of a house much larger than his own but only a mile or so east of it. A moment later, he was holding his pistol in one hand and cocking it with the other. For the silence had been broken by the clanging of the door-bell.

Staring through a lace-curtained window, Peace made out two silhouettes above the garden wall: the shape of helmets identified the silhouettes as const-ables, So, with the one at the front door, Peace had to contend with three policemen. Perhaps there were others. He wasn't too worried – a single pistol was a hell of a sight more use than a whole forest of truncheons.

Throwing open the window, he tumbled through and raced round the side of the house, away from the constables by the wall. But they were after him. He could hear the thud of their footsteps, their shouts.

He wheeled as a policeman tried to head him off. Then he stopped dead in his tracks, pointed the pistol at the nearest policeman, shouted: 'Keep off or I'll shoot you.' But the constable – his name was Edward Robinson – continued to advance.

Peace fired twice.

Both shots missed.

Robinson must afterwards have thanked the Lord that it was a wet night, because as he slipped and slid on the grass, two more bullets whistled past him.

Then he fell upon Peace, bearing him to the ground. Peace screamed: 'You bugger, I'll settle you this time.' There was a fifth explosion, and a bullet tore through Robinson's arm. Now, however, he was gripping the hand that gripped the gun. Peace moaned: 'Let me up – I'll go quietly.' And as he spoke, he eased a knife from an inside pocket of his coat. So Robinson gave him a few raps on the head with his truncheon, more than enough to induce unconsciousness.

The other policeman approached. Warily. Just to be on the safe side, the senior officer banged his truncheon on Peace's wrist before taking the pistol. He then told Robinson to go and get his wound dressed. By the time Robinson staggered away, Peace was conscious. 'I only did it to frighten him,' he explained.

He was less communicative at Greenwich Police station, and later in Newgate Gaol, refusing to give his name and pretending deafness when asked about his background and present address. But on 1 November, the inventive Henry Brion received a letter from someone calling himself John Ward, who requested the pleasure of his company – just for a short while – at Newgate. His curiosity aroused, Brion went to the prison, had a chat with 'John Ward' – and afterwards, still looking perplexed, told the police that the prisoner's 'real' name was John Thompson.

The house in Evelina Road was deserted, most of the fine accoutrements gone, when the police arrived there. However, Susan Bailey was quickly traced. Having been told that she would get off scot-free if she talked,

DEADLY STRUGGLE BETWEEN PEACE AND CONSTABLE ROBINSON.

she became a chatterbox, giving away all the secrets Charles had confided in her and, for good measure, directing the police to a house in Sheffield where they found not only Hannah and young Willie but a considerable quantity of loot.

The legal proceedings against Charles Peace were mere formalities. After he had been found guilty on a variety of counts relating to the crime in South London, he was indicted for the murder of Arthur Dyson.

During a train journey to Sheffield, where he was to appear at a magistrates' court, he attempted to dive out of a window – and, despite being handcuffed, very nearly succeeded. A warder managed to grab his ankle and hold on while the train raced along at fifty miles an hour and Peace tried to kick himself free. The train had travelled several miles when Peace's boot came off in the warder's hand, and he fell head-first on the side of the track. Until now, another warder and a commuter had been trying to budge the handle of the communication cord. At last, the handle moved and the train ground to a halt. The warders ran back along the track and found Peace lying where he had fallen. He afterwards insisted that the apparent bid to escape had in fact been an attempt at suicide, since he didn't fancy being launched into eternity by a hangman.

He recovered from his injuries soon enough to prevent any delay in his appearance at Leeds Assizes. Hurried through well within a day, the trial resulted in a verdict of guilty and the sentence of death, which was carried out exactly three weeks later, Peace by then having composed a memorial notice:

In Memory of Charles Peace
who was executed in Armley Prison
Tuesday, February 25th, 1879
Aged 47.
For that I don but never intended.

To increase the satisfactoriness of the ending, let me add that a few days prior to Charles Peace's brief encounter with William Marwood, the executioner, he dictated a detailed confession to the murder of Nicholas Cock, two and a half years before. William Habron, the young Irishman convicted of the crime, had been reprieved from hanging, and so was able to appreciate the free pardon that was granted.

The Demise of the Ice-Cream Blonde

Recently, when I was taking part in a radio programme, I was asked to say what makes a 'perfect murder'. Having put the question, the interviewer settled back, thinking that he could relax while I talked about some famous unsolved cases. But my answer was short and, to the interviewer, unexpected. I pointed out that the truly perfect murders are those we don't know about: not the headline-provoking cases, 'locked-room mysteries' and the like, in which the investigators, though probably sure in their minds of whodunit, are unable to find the clinching clue – but the cases that are never investigated, for the simple reason that no one realizes that murder has been committed.

I mentioned, in passing, that if present-day crime statistics are to be believed, then poisoning, the classic stealthy method of extinguishment, is virtually extinct – a notion that is hard to countenance, considering the increased availability of toxic substances. One man's prescription – for barbiturates or strong sleeping-pills, for instance – is another man's poison; in many, far too many, homes, the bathroom-cabinet or medicine-chest is crammed with the remains of remedies that, in the wrong hands, can be handy for homicide. No; it is not that poisoning has lost popularity – just that poisons more sophisticated than the old-fashioned arsenic or belladonna are making it simpler to commit the perfect murder.

Following the broadcast, I got a letter from a listener who wondered if I could think of any *near*-perfect murders: cases in which only initially or with no second thoughts, the police misconstrued murder as suicide or accident. Straightway, I thought of Evelyn Foster, the young hire-car driver who on Twelfth Night, 1931, was burnt to death at a place called Wolf's Nick on the Northumberland moors; before dying, she gave an account of how a passenger had attacked and set fire to her – but the local police, keen to hide their incompetence, insisted that she had taken her own life.

And then another case came into my mind – another case in which a car was the instrument of death.

The car, a convertible Pierce-Arrow, belonged to the film-star Thelma Todd, who was known as 'the ice-cream blonde', a description that had first been applied to her in 1925 or thereabouts, when she had worked as a fashion-model to pay for tuition as a school teacher. She was already teaching when she entered a beauty contest and won the title of 'Miss Massachusetts'. Her father, who was a politician, had prints made from a photograph of Thelma in her unmoistened swimming-costume, and distributed them among his friends, supporters and constituents. One of the receivers, the owner of a cinema, so liked what he saw that he got in touch with Jesse Lasky, the head of the Paramount film company, suggesting that Thelma ought to be in pictures.

Just at that time, Lasky was setting up a school for starlets at Paramount's eastern studios in New York City. He wrote to Thelma, inviting her to join the first class, and she accepted like a shot.

For six months, she and a score of other young hopefuls took lessons in make-up, literary pedestrian-ism (which was a matter of walking without tilting a slim volume from the head), fencing, horse-riding, social and studio etiquette, ballroom dancing, smiling, dealing with fan-mail, car-driving, choosing garb appropriate to various Occasions – and even, just occasionally, acting. In March 1926, she received a one-year contract, and subsequently she played parts – small at first, but gradually growing in importance – in films ranging from musicals to melodramas, from cowboy adventures to comedies.

It was as a comedienne that she caught the roving eye of Hal Roach, who lured her from Paramount to his production company in Hollywood. For a year or two, she worked almost without a break, playing leads opposite Laurel and Hardy, Harry Langdon, and other comedy stars. Then, having chosen to be a freelance, she appeared in a number of high-budget productions, including the first screen-version of Dashiell Hammett's *The Maltese Falcon*, with Bebe Daniels, and two Margaret-Dumontless Marx Brothers farces.[1] In 1931, she returned to Hal Roach's company to make a series of comedies with ZaSu Pitts, the dithery star who had concocted her first name from the names of two

1. In *The Comic Mind: Comedy and the Movies (London, 1974)*, Gerald Mast writes: 'Thelma Todd … is the sexual siren – blonde, curvaceous, young, pretty, and no purer than she ought to be. When Groucho romances her, his object is more pleasure than business. They dance the tango in Thelma's stateroom in *Monkey Business*. In fact, they dance it on her bed. And in *Horse Feathers* Thelma plays a parody of blonde sexuality in general and Jean Harlow specifically – including the famed beauty spot (which wanders from cheek to cheek and is inconsistently present from take to take). In this film, Thelma pulls the reversal on Groucho; she pretends to romance him, but is really intent on using her sexuality to get something away from him. In a specific parody of Harlow in *Dinner at Eight*, Todd begs Groucho to let her see the "secret signals" for the big football game, using Harlow's baby talk and baby whine as her means of turning sex into tool.

'But Groucho is not one to be taken in by romantic drivel. As they glide along in a canoe (Thelma rows, Groucho merely sits and plays his ukelele), he listens to Thelma's baby talk, glances at a fake-looking duck idyllically swimming beside the canoe, and asks: "Did that come out of you or the duck?" When she continues with her baby talk, he responds in the same language: How would she wike him to push his big foot wight down her widdle thwoat? So much for sex symbols and romance.'

The *Marx Brothers Scrapbook* (London, 1974) contains the

favourite aunts, *Eliza* and *Susan*. The series pleased the
public, and early in 1933, when the last of the films was
completed, Thelma signed up for a similar series with
Patsy Kelly (who turned out to be one of Hollywood's
'survivors': thirty-five years later, she played a cameo
part in the horror movie *Rosemary's Baby*).
mary's Baby).

Thelma's screen persona in the films with ZaSu Pitts
and Patsy Kelly seems to have been similar to her real
personality: a good-time girl who liked playing practical jokes, attending parties, and indulging in casual
love-affairs. And so it came as a surprise to her friends
when, in the early summer of 1932, she married her
agent, a man as unctuous as his name, which was
Pasquale Di Cicci. The friends were not at all surprised
that the marriage did not endure. In March 1934,
Thelma obtained a divorce on the grounds of cruelty
and incompatibility.

Within weeks of the divorce, her friends were
wondering if she would ever learn, for her constant
escort to night-clubs and parties was Roland West,

---

transcript of interviews between the compilers, Groucho Marx
and Richard J. Anobile. Extract:

GROUCHO: ... You know who I thought was cute?
Thelma Todd. She worked in a couple of our pictures. I
wanted to fuck her.
ANOBILE: Who decided to replace Margaret Dumont with
Todd?
GROUCHO: Well, I don't know. I guess Maggie just didn't
fit in those pictures. So we had Thelma Todd, who I was
trying to fuck. We had a scene in *Horse Feathers* where we
were on a boat on a lake. I think it was a canoe and I was
sitting on one end and she was on the other. According to
the script she was supposed to be trying to get plans from
me for the football game or something. Well, nobody
asked her if she could swim and at one point she fell
overboard and into the lake. She kept hollering for help,
but I thought she was kidding. Six stage hands ended up
jumping into the lake to rescue her ... She was a beauty.

once a a busy film-director but now considered a has-been; aged forty-seven, he had not made a picture since 1931, and there seemed little likelihood that he would ever direct again.

Then Thelma gave everyone – well, lots of people – another surprise by opening a beach-restaurant near Santa Monica, the resort-town to the north of Holly-wood, and appointing Roland West as manager. Seeking to cash in on her fame, she called the place Thelma Todd's Roadside Rest. She and West lived on the first floor – in separate apartments, so it was said – and, for some reason that seems never to have been explained, West also had a cottage high on the hill that overlooked the restaurant.

Part of the ground floor of the cottage had been converted to a two-car garage, and it was there that Thelma kept her Pierce-Arrow. An odd arrangement, that. After all, at the rear of the restaurant – that is, on the seaward side – was a shack that could easily have been turned into a garage; and though the cottage was no more than 400 feet from the restaurant, it could only be reached from there by climbing 270 rough steps – dusty in dry weather, muddy in wet – that were cut into the steep hill.

When the dead body of Thelma Todd was found in the garage, the police were flummoxed why such a wealthy woman, who had often worn expensive and delicate clothes – usually in white or strawberry-pink, enhancing the noticeableness of her ice-cream blonde-ness, albeit in a sundae sort of way – had put up with having to ascend the hill whenever she needed her car, to wobble vertiginously down it after stowing the machine: a tidy act that was often made complex by pitch-darkness, weariness, and wooziness induced by the mixing of mixed drinks called cocktails. It was one among sundry puzzles that, added together, would cause the head of the Santa Monica police department to complain of 'a mighty mysterious mystery'.

With the approach of Christmas 1935, Thelma Todd seemed to have every reason for feeling contented with life. The thirty-year-old star had two movies, *All-American Toothache* and *Bohemian Girl*, awaiting release, and she had recently signed a new contract with Hal Roach that would earn her $1500 a week. The beach-restaurant was making money under the management of Roland West – and, so she said, she was glad to get away from Hollywood each night, or most of them, to stay in her apartment above the restaurant. The fact that she now lived on the coast did not inhibit her sociability: three or four times a week, she either attended a party in the film capital or entertained at the Roadside Rest. And she had told friends of a 'marvellous romance' that she was having with a San Francisco businessman.

Back in August, she had been irritated rather than frightened when she received a number of extortion notes, one threatening that her restaurant would be 'blown up' if she didn't part with $10,000. Treating the threats as an occupational hazard, she had referred them to the Federal Bureau of Investigation, and soon afterwards a young man residing near the Paramount film studios in New York City had been arrested. He had willingly confessed – though bafflingly, for his explanation for the threats was that he had been madly in love with Thelma Todd since first seeing her on the screen – and he was now confined in a mental institution.

Stanley Lupino, the English comedian, was another of Thelma's fans. When he came to Hollywood to visit his daughter, the actress Ida Lupino, she arranged a party at the Trocadero restaurant, one of the few swell-elegant places in the vicinity, with Thelma as guest of honour. One of the twenty or so people who got invitations must have mentioned the forthcoming occasion to Pasquale Di Cicci, Thelma's former husband. Shortly before the party, which was to be held on the evening of Saturday, 14 December, Di Cicci happened to meet Ida Lupino. He asked her why he had not been invited. While she was fumbling for a polite explanation, he told her that he would like to come. And so she invited him.

The party was in full swing when Di Cicci turned up, wearing a tail-coat made from a substance that reflected light as efficiently as did his patent-leather pumps and his patent-leather hair. Adding acid to the lemon of embarrassment, he brought a comely young actress named Margaret Lindsay with him.

Ida Lupino afterwards recalled: 'He and Thelma spoke, but she was very indignant. She berated him bitterly for slighting me and herself.'

Di Cicci, with his less dazzling companion, retreated to another table. Thelma soon forgot the incident, or rather, put it out of her mind, and for the next few hours was the life and soul of the party.

But at about 2 a.m., something happened – something that was never explained – that wiped the smile from Thelma's face. Seated at an adjacent table were four men, one of whom was Sidney Grauman, the cinema magnate whose most famous property was the ornate Chinese Theatre on Hollywood Boulevard, the forecourt of which was indented with footprints, palm-impressions and autographs of movie personalities. Thelma walked over to the table and talked for some minutes with Grauman – and perhaps with his acquaintances. The actor Arthur Prince, one of Ida Lupino's guests, noted that 'when Thelma came back, she was totally different. All her gaiety had evaporated. She seemed terribly depressed.'

Shortly afterwards, the party broke up. Thelma had ordered a hire-car, and as soon as she got into it, she told the driver, Ernest Peters, to drive to Santa Monica at top speed 'because she feared that she might be kidnapped or slain by gangsters'. Had she not been a frequent customer, Peters would have sacrificed courtesy to cowardice and ordered her out of his limousine; instead, fearing for his own life as much as she feared for hers, he drove at between 65 and 70 miles an hour, reaching the Roadside Rest at about 3.30.

As Peters drove off, heading back to Hollywood at a more sedate speed, he glanced in the rear-mirror and saw that Thelma was still standing outside the restaurant.

He may have been the last person to see her alive.

The following evening – Sunday – four people who had attended Ida Lupino's party arrived at the Roadside Rest, looking forward to a slap-up meal. During the party, Thelma had made a wager with them, and, having lost, offered to pay her stake in the form of a free dinner at her restaurant. But the Roadside Rest was closed, and no amount of banging at any of the doors brought a response. Disappointed and, if the truth were known, a mite angry with Thelma for her forgetfulness (as they thought), the foursome sought food and booze elsewhere.

When Thelma's black maid, May Whitehead, let herself in on the Monday morning, she found to her surprise that her mistress's apartment on the first floor was empty, the bed still made up, apparently as she had left it two days before. Looking through the window at Roland West's cottage on the hill, she observed that the sliding door of the garage was partly open. Though she didn't fancy the steep climb, she decided that she had better investigate.

Edging into the garage, she saw Thelma sprawled across the driver's seat of her car, her head lolling against the steering wheel. She was dressed in the fur-coat, sequinned evening gown and blue satin shoes she had worn to the party. Blood blemished her pale face and stained the seat and the running-board of the car. She had been dead for some hours.

How long?

Since about 5 a.m. on Sunday, according to the

estimate of Dr A.F. Wagner, the county autopsy surgeon, who examined the body after the police, called to the scene by May Whitehead, had taken photographs.

Dr Wagner believed that the blood on Thelma's face 'probably resulted from wounds incurred when she crumpled in her car, her head striking the steering wheel'. He also reported: 'The autopsy showed monoxide poison, to the extent of 70 per cent of total saturation, in her blood. There may have been other contributing causes, but that was definitely the main factor. The fumes were breathed accidentally. Either she went to sleep with the motor running or she was overcome before she could help herself.'

The surgeon's findings and opinions seemed to put an end to the matter. Thelma Todd had died from an unfortunate accident. The notion that she might have committed suicide crossed some people's minds – but there was no last note, nothing that suggested a reason.

It wasn't long, however, before Dr Wagner's cut and dried report – especially the part dealing with the time of death – was being contradicted. And in no time at all, rumours began to scuttle around Hollywood. The strongest of them suggested why, and even on whose orders, the 'ice-cream blonde' might have been murdered.

The first doubts about the time of death arose from a statement made by the wife of the pudgy-faced film-actor Wallace Ford. Hearing that Dr Wagner (a name that everyone pronounced unmusically) had estimated that Thelma had died round about five on the Sunday morning, Martha Ford exclaimed:

'Nonsense!

'I'm positive, beyond all question, that I talked to her on the phone *between four o'clock and 4.30 on Sunday afternoon*. I've known her for years, and I couldn't be mistaken. I had invited her to a cocktail party celebrating my wedding anniversary. Her maid telephoned Saturday to say she would come.

'Sunday afternoon, she telephoned me. "It's Thelma, your hot toddy," she said. That was a nickname she liked to call herself. She said, "Darling, do you mind if I bring a guest?" I replied, "Of course not. Who is it?" "You'd never guess, and you'll be surprised when you see," she replied. I told her I was dying of curiosity, but she wouldn't tell me anything more.

'Then she said, "Oh, and another thing – I went to a party last night and I'm still in evening clothes. Do you mind?" I laughed and said she could come in anything she wanted, but to hurry. Then she hung up. I just couldn't understand it when she didn't arrive.'

In addition to this strong ear-witness evidence, there was eye-witness evidence from several people who claimed to have seen Thelma on the Sunday.

For instance, William Persson was sure that the actress had come into his cigar store in downtown Los Angeles, thirty miles from Santa Monica, *at nine in the morning*.

'I was struck by her beauty. I noticed that her high-heeled blue shoes were a little bit dirty. She seemed unsteady on her feet, and I first thought she had a hangover. Then I decided that she was just nervous.

'She gave me a nickel and asked me to call a number for her. I don't remember the prefix, but the number was 7771. A minute or so later, a man came in and they left together. The man was cold sober. I can name two customers who also saw Miss Todd.'

Prolonging Thelma's life, Roland West's estranged wife Carmen declared that she had seen her in Hollywood *at about eleven o'clock on the Sunday night*:

'It was at Sunset Boulevard and Vine Street. She was in an automobile with a dark-complexioned, foreign-looking man whom I did not recognize.'

What of Roland West himself? Could he throw any

light on why Thelma, arriving back at the Roadside Rest in the early hours of Sunday, had traipsed up the steep hill to the garage instead of entering her apartment above the restaurant?

He said that, on the Saturday evening, just before Thelma left to attend Ida Lupino's party, he had told her to be back by 2 a.m. – at which time he would lock the doors and go to bed. 'She said, smiling, "Five minutes after two." I said, "Two o'clock." She said right back, "Five minutes after two," and we repeated this several times. It was all in a joking way.'

Shortly before two, he had received a telephone call from Sid Grauman, the cinema tycoon, saying that Thelma was on her way home. He had waited half an hour, then locked up and gone to bed. If Thelma, on her return, had banged on the doors to be let in, he had not heard her; nor, it seemed, had her dog, a bull-terrier called White Flash, which had not barked in the night.

If it was accepted that both Roland West and White Flash were sound sleepers, the ex-director's story held a possible solution to one of the main mysteries of the case: the *setting* of Thelma Todd's death. Finding herself locked out, had she gone to the garage, turned on the ignition of her car for warmth additional to that provided by her fur-coat, fallen asleep ... and been poisoned by the carbon-monoxide fumes from the exhaust? Well, perhaps. The theory was blunted by a statement from May Whitehead, who said that, without West's knowledge, she had given Thelma a spare key to the back door of the restaurant, and that Thelma had kept the key in her purse.

The mystery of why Thelma had gone to the garage was complicated by a puzzle as to how she had got there. The police, for once acting efficiently, carried out an experiment. They got a woman of Thelma's build, wearing shoes similar to those worn by the actress, to climb the 270 steps up the hill. The satin shoes were more scuffed than Thelma's, which suggested that she had not made the long climb.

When the police eventually thought to inquire whether anyone lived in Roland West's cottage on the hill, they learned that the bedroom directly above the garage was occupied by the bookkeeper-cum-cashier at the Roadside Rest, a seventy-year-old man named Charles Smith. The likelihood that Mr Smith had heard something that could be construed as a clue was increased by the fact that there was a sizeable hole in the ceiling of the garage. The trouble was that Mr Smith was nowhere to be found. The police, who were already discommoded by the disappearance of Pasquale Di Cicci (after a couple of days as a missing person, he showed up in New York, explaining that he had 'departed Los Angeles on an unplanned business trip before the tragic news of Thelma's passing was made public'), enlisted the help of the press in tracing Mr Smith – who, after a couple of days as a missing person, showed up in Santa Monica, complaining that 'it is a downright lie that I have been missing: I was visiting with kin, and they will confirm that I was no more missing than they were'. Asked to cast his mind back to the early hours of Sunday, he said, 'I was resting at that time in my normal place of rest, namely the room over the garage in my employer's cottage', and stifled further questions by adding: 'I am an old man, and I go to sleep the moment my head dents the pillow. If Miss Todd came to the garage, opened the door and started the car, she did it quietly. I heard nothing – not a peep.'

On Wednesday, 18 December, an inquest jury weighed Dr Wagner's evidence against the extra-legal testimony in the papers, and returned the following verdict:

Thelma Alice Todd Di Cicci came to her death December 15, 1935, in a garage at 17531 Posetano

Road, near Santa Monica, California, and, from the evidence submitted, death appears to have been accidental – but we recommend further investigation by the proper authorities.

Though there was talk of 'icing the cadaver', in case the proper authorities wanted to check upon something, it was cremated on Thursday. The New York *Times* reckoned that, in the morning,

> twelve thousand persons walked past Miss Todd's orchid-satin bier, where the body, clad in blue satin lounging pyjamas, lay in state for five hours preceding the funeral at Forest Lawn Memorial Park. There was a profusion of flowers. In the centre of the chapel, on a table, was a photograph of Miss Todd.
>
> The funeral services, private, were held in the Wee Kirk o' the Heather, in Glendale, the church where the funerals of Will Rogers, Marie Dressler and other screen celebrities have been held.

A grand-jury investigation was ordered. While this was going on, several members of the jury told the press that they suspected foul play, and the foreman coined the term, 'the monoxide murder case'. But after weeks of puzzling over the evidence, the grand jury gave up trying to establish whether Thelma Todd had died by accident, committed suicide, or been murdered. They announced the non-verdict of 'death due to carbon monoxide poisoning', and left it at that.

It is hard to think of another case of suspicious death in which so many questions that should – could – have been answered were left dangling. This was partly due to police ineptitude. Only partly. Certain facts – some of them known to some policemen – were covered up. There is little doubt that the cover-up was organized, and paid for, by bosses of the motion-picture industry – men more concerned about box-office receipts than about truth and justice, willing to go to any lengths to avert a scandal. They had been responsible for cover-ups in the past; they would be responsible for others in the future.

To pick out just a few of the unanswered questions: Was a key to the back door of the Roadside Rest found in Thelma's purse? Indeed, was the *purse* found? Was Dr Wagner correct in his belief that the blood on Thelma's face 'resulted from wounds incurred when ... her head struck the steering wheel'? (Though, of course, possible, nine times out of ten a head lolling on to a steering wheel would not produce even a bruise, let alone an open wound.) It was said in the first police report that there was blood 'on the seat' – but no indication was given as to whether the blood was actually *on* the seat or at the side. If it was on the seat, beneath Thelma's body, then the steering-wheel explanation for the facial wound was surely ruled out: she must have suffered the injuries before she either entered or was bundled into the car.

Was Thelma Todd murdered? I believe so. And it seems to me that the motive for the crime might have been discovered if the police had investigated an incident during Ida Lupino's party.

The morning after Thelma's body was found, Alexander Hounie, the head waiter at the Trocadero, received a card on which was pasted words clipped from a newspaper: 'With*HOLD* testimony – *OR* kidnap trip'. That night, as he was driving home, he was forced to the kerb by another car, and one of the two men inside shouted threats at him. What were the threateners worried about? Surely not that Hounie might have seen something. More likely that he might have caught a snatch of conversation during his peregrinations between the tables. Was it thought that he had overheard an explanation for the actress's death?

You will recall that, towards the end of Ida Lupino's

party, Thelma walked over to the table occupied by Sid Grauman and three unidentified men. When she returned to her own table, she was very depressed. Soon afterwards, if Roland West is to be believed, Grauman phoned him to say that Thelma was on her way back to the Roadside Rest. It is impossible to believe that Thelma asked Grauman, one of the most powerful figures in Hollywood, to act as a messenger-boy. So what was the true reason for the phone call?

Grauman may or may not have had business associations with the Mafia, but he certainly numbered several mobsters among his acquaintances, and his three companions at the Trocadero may have been employees at the California branch of Charles 'Lucky' Luciano's New-York-based corporation of crime. Prohibition had recently been repealed, bringing to an end the lucrative trade in illicit booze, and Charles Luciano (let us call him that, though his real name was Salvatore Lucania) was 'muscling in' on gambling. Shortly before the party at the Trocadero, Thelma – in the presence of her lawyer Ronald Button – had turned down an offer from one of Luciano's men to take over the top storey of the Roadside Rest and turn it into a casino. If the subject arose again at Grauman's table at the Trocadero, and if Thelma again said no, Grauman could have had a reason for telephoning Roland West, if only to advise him to make himself scarce before Thelma returned. And, of course, Thelma would have had a good reason for telling the hire-car driver, Ernest Peters, that 'she feared that she might be kidnapped or slain by gangsters'.

I don't know what your conclusion is, but I am pretty sure that Thelma Todd, the 'ice-cream blonde', was the victim of a 'perfect murder' committed by a relatively sophisticated hit-man for the Mafia.

The Curious Case of the Queer Customer

By no means all show-business people accept that there is any truth in the saying, probably coined by an inefficient press agent, that 'bad publicity is the best publicity'. Perhaps, to misquote the show-business academic Cyril Joad, it depends what one means by *bad*. Naughtiness may add a pinch of ersatz spice to a bland personality; in some areas of the entertainment industry – those associated with pop music, for instance – minor breaches of the law may give a false sheen of glamour to the offstage activities of performers who need sequins on their costumes so as to shine.

No discussion of the help or hindrance of bad publicity to a stage career would be complete without reference to the experience of the actor Philip Yale Drew, who, in the latter half of 1929, was cast by the police as the villain in a real-life murder melodrama, causing him to miss several performances of a touring production of a thriller called *The Monster*.

I am old-fashioned enough to believe that a story – or, for that matter, a play – should have a beginning, a middle, and an end; and in that order. But the scenario of the Reading Murder Case must, I think, start off with what should really be Act One, Scene *Two*. The first scene, quite long and largely depending for its effect on how well a large number of cameo parts are portrayed, has to be a flashback.

So ... Act One, Scene Two.

The setting: a tobacconist's shop in Cross Street, a short thoroughfare of shops and residences that runs between two of the main streets in Reading, Berkshire.

The time: six o'clock on the evening of Saturday, 22 June 1929.

The proprietor of the shop, sixty-year-old Alfred Oliver, sat behind the counter. On Monday, all being well, he and his wife Annie would be starting a week's holiday in Devon. He had bought the return-tickets to Teignmouth at the railway station just up the road, and, feeling extravagant, had paid a shilling for a Great Western Railway pamphlet entitled *Through the Window: Paddington to Penzance*.

Now, in this quiet part of the day, half an hour from closing time, he flicked through the pages of the pamphlet, anticipating the visual delights of the journey to the seaside.

Within ten minutes or so, the little book was lying on the floor, its cover dappled with spots of blood. Much else was marred by blood: the centre of the counter, the glass cases displaying and keeping dust off cigars and pipes, the neatly-ranked packets of cigarettes and tobacco on the shelves. The blood, pints of it, had gushed and splashed from twenty-one lacerated wounds on the head of Mr Oliver, who was sitting untidily on the floor behind the counter.

At about a quarter past six, Annie Oliver came into the shop after taking her Pekingese for a walk. Perhaps she at once saw the blood and noted that the cash-register was open – if she did, her surprise at finding the shop apparently unattended prevented messages of danger from shouting in her mind. She went to the counter. She saw the huddled figure. She ran to the Welcome Café, a few doors away, and cried out to her friend Nellie Taylor to come quickly: 'Something's happened to Olly.'

Amazingly, Alfred Oliver was still alive. Even more amazingly, he was conscious – able to speak, to try to answer the questions put to him by his wife, the several neighbours who came into the shop, and an off-duty constable who had happened to be purchasing a weekend joint from a nearby butcher. But all Oliver could say about the attack was 'I remember reading ... then nothing more.'

An ambulance having been called, he was taken to the Royal Berkshire Hospital. There he died almost exactly twenty-four hours after the attack. By then, the local police were treating the crime as murder; the chief constable had requested help from Scotland Yard, and two members of the 'murder squad' were travelling to Reading.

Both of the detectives, Chief Inspector James Berrett and Sergeant John Harris, were immense: well over six-feet tall and big with it. Berrett was an especially impressive sight. A dandy, usually favouring a cravat instead of a neck-tie, he sported a heavy but meticulously curried beard; his bushy eyebrows were almost as large as his moustache. He and Harris were reckoned to be the Yard's most formidable team, a reputation that stemmed chiefly from their success a year before, when they had caught Frederick Browne and William Kennedy, the thugs who had killed Police Constable George Gutteridge in an Essex lane and then put a bullet through each of his eyes in the superstitious belief that the retinas of a murder victim retain the image of the killer or killers.

The Reading police already knew – or thought they knew – the motive for the crime in Cross Street: the 'no-sale' button had been pressed to open the cash-register, and all the bank-notes stolen – about ten pounds'–worth, according to Mrs Oliver. The police had also heard the first of several reports of a strange man acting strangely in the vicinity of the shop during the afternoon preceding the murder.

As more eye-witnesses came forward, Berrett made an incomplete chronology of how the man had spent the afternoon:

1.30. The man spoke to William Loxton, one of the

butchers in the shop close to the tobacconist's. 'He didn't come in,' Loxton stated, 'but asked, "Have you any calves' liver?" Before I could say yes or no, he went away. I said to the other man in the shop, "That gentleman's a bit of a lad. He's either a Scotchman or an Irishman. At any rate, he's not an Englishman."'

2–2.40. Between these times, Sydney Turnbull, an estate agent working from premises opposite Oliver's shop, saw the man 'staggering about in the vicinities of the Welcome Café and the International Tea Co.'s stores at No. 25. I thought he was under the influence of drink.'

3.30–4. Mrs Winifred Greenwood was shopping in Friar Street, one of the main thoroughfares connected by Cross Street, making an H, when she noticed 'a man staggering a bit, walking with his hands in his pockets, and with his coat under his arm, dragging on the ground'.

4.15–5. Nellie Taylor, of the Welcome Café, served a meal to a man 'who spoke with good English at times, then lapsed into a very strong American accent; he was in an advanced state of drunkenness'. He ordered four fried eggs, two rashers, rolls and butter, and a cup of tea. When Mrs Taylor presented the bill, the man searched his pockets 'for three or four minutes' before finding some silver wrapped in a ten-shilling note. As he was leaving, he asked: 'Does this street lead to the County Theatre?' No one answered, so he repeated the question. 'Straight up the street and turn to the left,' Mrs Taylor told him, and he said, 'Thank God somebody has answered me', as he lurched out of the café.

4.40. According to Thomas Windle, a sanitary inspector, this was the time when he saw a drunken man gazing around at the buildings in Cross Street, then entering the Welcome Café. (Clearly, either Windle got the time wrong or Nellie Taylor was wildly astray about the time when the man came into the café

– or there were two strange men in Cross Street.)

5.15. George Nicholson, a gardener, bought some tobacco from Alfred Oliver, then walked up the street to wait for his wife, who was in the International Tea Co.'s store. 'A man passed me. He had his mack on his arm, dragging along the pavement. He was staggering, and reeled off the pavement on to a stationary car. He got to the lamp-post near Oliver's and appeared to be counting with his fingers all down the lamp to the bottom. Then he threw the mackintosh over his shoulder and walked into Friar Street.'

5.30. Mrs Kathleen Earl, on her way to the butcher's, saw 'a man walking in the middle of the road, behaving in a very peculiar way, muttering to himself and looking at the windows of the shops'.

5.30–6. William Loxton, the butcher, saw the man who, about four hours before, had inquired about calves' liver. Now 'he was by Bradley's wireless shop, opposite Oliver's. He was coming towards my shop. Then he stopped, turned, and went towards Mr Oliver's shop. He appeared to be very agitated and undecided. After that, I lost sight of him.'

Apart from a few minor variations, the descriptions of the man tallied. He was dressed in dark clothes. He was quite tall, middle-aged, and had iron-grey hair.

Who was he? Where was he now?

Actually, the eye-witnesses' accounts contained several possible clues to both questions. It is surprising that Inspector Berrett didn't notice them.

Nearly a month went by. On 19 July, the chief constable of Reading was in his club. A fellow-member approached him and casually suggested that 'the chap you're looking for is Philip Yale Drew, the actor fellow who was in *The Monster* at the County Theatre that week'.

The chief constable telephoned Detective Sergeant Harris who, in turn, rang Berrett. Other bells began ringing – in the minds of the two Scotland Yard men.

Harris made inquiries, and learned that *The Monster* was still traipsing round the provinces. That week, the production was at St. Helens, in Lancashire, and on Monday it would start a run at the Palace Theatre at Trent Bridge, Nottingham.

Further inquiries revealed that Philip Yale Drew was still with the company, playing the same part that he had played in Reading during the week that ended with a murder. The part was that of a clever detective.

Philip Yale Drew was forty-nine, and had been an actor for thirty years, when he became the leading suspect in the Reading Murder Case.

To many people, film-fans as well as theatregoers, he was better known as 'Young Buffalo' than by his real name, which had been bestowed on him when he was born in the village of Marshfield Hills, Massachusetts, the third child of a couple who ran a small hotel. He was precociously adept at riding and training horses, and his equestrian knacks, nurtured by a period as a ranch-hand in the wilds of Nebraska, led to his first break in the theatre: billed as 'Young Buffalo', he toured the country in one cowboy melodrama after another – presumably in theatres with reinforced stages, for the plots of the plays were always interrupted by 'specialty scenes' when he appeared on horseback to demonstrate what the posters termed 'the unbelievable communion betwixt man and beast'.

One gathers that he was a less impressive performer when standing on his own feet. Even so, in 1910 a matinée of *King of the Wild West* was attended by Ellen Terry, who was herself touring America, and she afterwards visited Drew in his dressing-room and suggested that British audiences would be drawn by the novelty of a production featuring a man-and-steed double-act. Excited by the idea, Drew persuaded his backer to start making arrangements, and in September of that year the entire company – including 'Major, the

Wonder Horse' – set sail for London.

The British tour of *King of the Wild West* was a great success, breaking box-office records at many theatres, and Philip Yale Drew, 'Young Buffalo', became a celebrity. The toured lasted for three years. The only trouble was that, in return for the display of an advertisement for White Horse Whisky in a saloon scene, the distillers sent four quarts of Scotch to Drew's hotel each week – and before long he was not only consuming the liquor but sending out for more.

When the tour ended, he appeared in music-halls in a sketch called 'The Cowboy and the Girl'. Then he wrote and produced *The Frozen North* – and lost a lot of money, chiefly because war was declared shortly after the play opened. Undeterred, Drew put together another production, of a drama called *The Texas Ranger* – and lost even more money.

He used up the last of his savings on a steerage-class steamship ticket to America and a couple of crates of whisky. After spending a few weeks in Marshfield Hills, he travelled west – to Hollywood. There, he starred in half a dozen films: *Tex of the Timberlands* was one; *The Hobo of Pizen City* another. Film-making did not appeal to him, however; he longed to get back to the stage – and, despite his last two unfortunate experiences, to the *British* stage. Once he had saved what he thought was sufficient money, he sailed back to England, arriving in London early in 1920. And he struck lucky at once, being engaged for a leading role in a West End production of a cowboy play. For the next three years, he appeared under the same management in similar plays, London runs being preceded and followed by tours.

But by now the years of heavy drinking were starting to show, mottling his features and thickening his jowls; though he was only in his early forties, the 'Young Buffalo' image was a thing of the past. Drink had not affected his ability to learn lines, but he became increasingly unreliable offstage, turning up late to rehearsals, having to be chaperoned at the end of a week in one town to ensure that he caught the train to the next, and treating newspaper reporters with scant respect. Eventually, the London manager decided that enough was enough, and Drew spent some months 'resting'. What made things worse for him was that the vogue of cowboy plays seemed to be over, killed by wild-west movies starring men like Tom Mix and William S. Hart.

Modifying his native accent, and wearing worsted rather than buckskin, he appeared in small parts in repertory theatres and in touring productions playing the 'No. 2 dates'. Towards the end of 1927, he obtained the script of a thriller entitled *The Monster*, which included a showy part – just right for him, he thought – of a detective called 'Red' Mackenzie. He showed the script to a successful young actress, Olga Lindo, who agreed to finance a touring production run by her parents, Frank and Marion, and with Drew as the detective. *The Monster* opened at the New Theatre, Cardiff, early in the following year, and then began what turned out to be a long trek around No. 2 – or even No. 3 – dates in towns up and down the country: among other places, Torquay, Aberdeen, Liverpool, Malvern, Grimsby, Rochdale ... and, in the week ending Saturday, 22 June 1929, Reading.

The Monster was midway through its run at the Palace Theatre, Trent Bridge, Nottingham, when Philip Yale Drew was visited at his digs by Detective Sergeant Harris, who invited him to the local police station to answer questions relating to the murder of Alfred Oliver in Reading on 22 June.

'Murder!' Drew exclaimed. 'I don't know where I was that day. Are you accusing me?'

'I am accusing no one,' Harris replied. 'Will you come to the station?'

'Sure,' Drew said calmly.

At the station, after being cautioned, he was interrogated for three hours. He agreed that, just to while away the time until the evening performances, he must have sauntered around the centre of Reading on the Saturday – but, he said, he had no recollection of being in Cross Street, and he had certainly not entered Alfred Oliver's shop.

Sergeant Harris told Drew that he could leave, adding that he would probably have to be questioned again. As soon as Drew had gone, Harris carefully lifted a sheet of paper that he had got the actor to handle, and had the fingerprints compared with a print that had been found on a blood-drenched display-case at the scene of the crime. The prints did not match.

Later that day, however, Harris's disappointment evaporated. Since the Reading police had obtained statements from the half-dozen people who had seen a strange man acting strangely in Cross Street between about half-past one and six on the day of the murder, a seemingly more important eye-witness, Mrs Alice James, had reluctantly come forward. While Harris was questioning Drew, she was being driven to Nottingham. In the early evening, she stood with a plain-clothes officer near the stage-door of the Palace Theatre. As soon as she saw Drew approaching, she tapped the policeman on the arm, signifying that Drew was the man she had seen in the doorway of the tobacconist's shop, *wiping blood from his face*, at about ten minutes past six on Saturday, 22 June.

Mrs James's evidence, though impressive, was not considered sufficient to justify an arrest. And so the investigators tried to build a case that would stand up in court. It must have been the most itinerant investigation ever: as *The Monster* moved from town to town – from Nottingham to North Shields to St. Albans, then west for week-long engagements at places in Wales – one or more of the detectives followed.

Several times their hopes were raised – then dashed. They learned that, prior to the week in Reading, Drew had been seen with a walking-stick, ornately carved and with a silver handle. He didn't use it now. What had become of it? Though none of the people who had seen the strange man in Cross Street had mentioned a stick when describing him, could it be the missing murder-weapon? A detective asked Drew about the stick, and was told that it had 'gone missing', perhaps left in a pub or on a train, before the visit to Reading. The police tried hard to disprove this assertion, but unfruitfully.

Then there was The Mystery of the Disappearing Trousers. According to Drew, he had put the trousers of his blue suit, with three pounds in one of the pockets, in his basketwork skip after the final performance in Reading. When he got to the next town, Maidstone, the trousers were missing. He reported his loss to Marion Lindo, who went to the trouble of writing to the manager of the Royal County Theatre, Reading. The police, of course, suspected that Drew had not mislaid the trousers but had destroyed them because they were spattered with Alfred Oliver's blood.

However, when *The Monster* company arrived in St. Albans, Mrs Lindo happened to go into Drew's dressing-room – and saw the blue trousers draped over a corner of his skip. Drew, after expressing amazement that the trousers had turned up, informed the police. A detective came to the theatre, established that the trousers were of the same material as the jacket, and extracted from the pockets, not three pounds, but about thirty-five shillings in notes and change, a key, a booklet of postage-stamps, a good-luck telegram, a hand-bill advertising *The Monster*, three buttons and a collar-stud. The detective couldn't tell whether or not the trousers had recently been cleaned, but he was sure that the pockets were new. The complete suit was sent to an analyst, who failed to trace any blood on it. Still, the police remained suspicious – and became more so when they learnt that, before the visit to St. Albans, Drew had used cleaning fluid on the jacket.

But suspicion was a long way from proof. Chief Inspector Berrett and Sergeant Harris, moping at how their conjoined fame as the avengers of George Gutteridge was being tarnished by a damned actor, decided to pass the buck to Reading's coroner. It was agreed that the adjourned inquest should be resumed on Wednesday, 2 October. The coroner would be both inquisitor and judge – and, with luck, the jury would return a verdict of Guilty against the star-witness, Philip Yale Drew.

As the coroner's court was too small to accommodate the large number of witnesses, let alone the reporters and members of the public, the inquest was held in the oak-panelled magistrates' court.

The coroner, John Lancelot Martin, bald-headed and bespectacled, was determined to make the most of being a small fish transferred to a big pond. Actually, he made *too much* of it, delivering long and obviously prepared speeches, interrupting witnesses in mid-testimony, and, in trying to impress as a stiletto-sharp examiner, only succeeding in being domineering and rude. During the proceedings, he received much publicity, but not the sort he felt was his due: several reporters and editorial-writers criticized his behaviour. Rather than shining in the limelight, Martin, the silly little man, was singed by it.

Right at the start, when the murdered man's widow, Annie Oliver, was giving evidence, much of it tearfully, Martin made no secret of the fact that he shared the investigators' belief that Philip Yale Drew was responsible for her widowhood. 'Do you see anyone in this court,' he asked, 'who may have been in your shop as one of the customers on that particular Saturday?'

Who but Drew, sitting centre-stage on the first bench in the well of the court, flanked by the small figures of Frank and Marion Lindo, the producers of *The Monster*?

But after looking around the court, Mrs Oliver said – disappointingly so far as the coroner was concerned: 'No, I see no one.'

Still, the half-dozen witnesses – workers and shoppers in Cross Street – who had seen a 'queer customer' in the afternoon before the murder, all came up trumps for the 'prosecution', saying either that Drew was the man or that he strongly resembled him. Most importantly, Mrs Alice James, plump and reliable-looking, told of seeing a man standing in the doorway of the tobacconist's shop, wiping blood from his face, at about ten minutes past six, and when asked by Martin, 'Can you recognize anyone in this court as the man?', pointed at Drew, saying firmly, 'That is the man.'

By this time, the start of the second day of the inquest, Drew had been persuaded by a friend to engage lawyers to represent his interests. He had not needed much persuasion.

The evidence of the Cross-Street eye-witnesses, which, put into chronological sequence, placed Drew in the vicinity of the shop between 1.30 and 6.10, roughly the time of the murder, was called into question by several witnesses who testified to seeing him elsewhere at times during the same period. Marion Lindo, for instance:

'Mr Drew had lunch with my husband and I in our lodgings [across the road from Drew's digs] between 2 p.m. and 2.30. I couldn't say he was drunk, but my husband advised him to sleep for a little while on the sofa. I came to the sitting-room about four o'clock and woke him up. I noticed in his trouser-pocket the outline of what I took to be a whisky bottle. He denied that it was whisky, and refused to give it up. I asked several times, and I got very angry. He went out.

'I went over to his lodgings about ten minutes later. I found him lying down in his bedroom. I again asked for the bottle, and he said, "You can search where you like, but you won't find it." I searched but could not find it. Then his landlady told me that he had gone out. Just after five, near my lodgings, I saw Mr Drew. He was going home for tea. Later, I went to the theatre, where my dressing-room was next to Mr Drew's. The half-hour call that night would be at 6.20 for curtain-up at 6.50. I heard Mr Drew enter a few minutes before the call. At least, I took it to be him.'

Mrs Lindo's account was partly confirmed and to some extent amplified by Drew's landlady, Mrs Mary Goodall, a nervous, twittery-voiced woman who owned lots of clocks, all of which were either fast or slow. She recalled that 'it was between 3 p.m. and 3.30 when he returned [having lunched and napped at the Lindos' digs]. Mrs Lindo rushed in behind him. There were high words. I heard it all from downstairs. Then she came down. Whilst we were talking, Mr Drew came down and went out. He came back at a quarter past five, and I gave him a cup of tea. His hands were shaky and he spilt the greater part, some on his trousers and some on the floor. He was always more or less worse for what he had had, and he had had plenty,' She reckoned that he left for the theatre at ten past six – 'it might have been a minute or two later.'

A couple of the landlady's neighbours said that they had seen Drew running from the house some time after six, and several members of *The Monster* company swore that he was in the theatre before the half-hour call at 6.20.

Further doubt was cast on the Cross-Street witnesses' identification of Drew when his lawyer mentioned something that had not been disclosed by the police: a man bearing a striking resemblance to the actor had been in the centre of Reading just before and at the time of the murder. Interviewed by the police, he had satisfied them that he was innocent of the crime.

Now the big moment arrived. Philip Yale Drew left his seat and strode to the witness-box. Presumably tutored by his advisers, he underplayed his performance, and rarely fell into the trap of elongating his answers. Colleagues had spoken of his offstage unreliability, of his 'airy-fairyness', and he did not contradict them.

MARTIN: When did you first hear that a murder had been committed?
DREW: I simply don't know. Whenever it was, it didn't register. There have been other murders, but I do not read about them. There are quite enough worries and nerves without that.
MARTIN: You remember Saturday, 22 June?
DREW: I shall have to say that I never check times. I may be erratic, but I'm afraid I can't tell you, for instance, what time I left my lodgings. I feel I am at liberty to do as I like during the day. It is my business and nobody else's.

Asked about his earnings, he explained that he received four pounds a week plus a percentage of any profits: 'It is not easy to assess exactly, but in the neighbourhood of eighteen or twenty pounds.' If that was true, it seemed against the notion that he had killed Alfred Oliver in the furtherance of theft from the cash-register; in 1929, the pound was worth about twenty times what it is today.

Drew had the sense to appear as perplexed as the coroner when the subject arose of how the trousers of his suit had vanished soon after the murder, only to reappear seven weeks later, the seemingly new pockets containing less cash but many more odds and ends than he had mentioned when he had reported the loss of the garment.

All in all, he gave an assured performance in the witness-box. His fans in the public gallery, wanting him to put up a good show, were sure that he had done just that. At the end of the day, they hurried from the court to tell the crowds waiting outside that Philip, the wandering star who was 'one of the boys' when he was not being paid to act, had scored a triumph.

Next day (the seventh day of the inquest), John Lancelot Martin recapitulated the evidence, then sent the jury to their room to consider the verdict. After nearly three hours, they returned, and the foreman announced that they had come to the conclusion that the evidence was too conflicting to establish the guilt of any particular person: 'consequently, we return a verdict of wilful murder against some person or persons unknown.'

Drew smiled as the spectators went wild, cheering, clapping and shouting their congratulations. Afterwards, he needed assistance from the Reading constabulary to make his way through the cheering crowds that jammed the route from the court to his hotel. At last reaching the hotel – the Great Western, by the railway station – he hurried upstairs and stepped on to a balcony. The vast throng applauded. Drew raised his hands, first in a gesture of appreciation, then to indicate that he wanted silence for a curtain-speech.

'I want to thank you,' he declaimed, 'and to let you know how grateful I am for this wonderful demonstration. The prayers that have been sent up for me, and the glorious sympathy extended to me, have meant much. The One Above, like myself, knows that I have nothing to do with it in any way …. Good afternoon – and God bless you.'

As he waved and stepped out of sight, the cheers rose again. Even louder now. And so he took an encore.

He was made for life, it seemed. That evening and on the following day, newspapers throughout the country gave greater coverage to the verdict and the subsequent balcony scenes than they had given to the inquiry itself: Philip Yale Drew was front-page news, a household name, all set to re-establish himself as a *proper* star.

After some 'personal appearances' in music-halls and cinemas, he rejoined the *Monster* company, and there was talk of a London run. Only talk. A few weeks later, Frank and Marion Lindo announced that they were leaving the company. The apparent suddenness of their decision gave rise to a medley of rumours, some of which, carefully adapted so as to avoid libel, were referred to in press reports: *the Lindos had stuck by Drew during his ordeal, but they had known all along that he was the killer of Alfred Oliver – now, terrified by his drunken rages, they were not forsaking 'The Monster' but escaping from Drew.* It was pointed out that Drew had not been acquitted by the inquest jury: 'some person unknown' could be taken to mean a person against whom the evidence was not quite strong enough; the double-jeopardy rule did not apply to inquest verdicts, and some day, perhaps, the police would find the vital, unequivocal clue, proving the actor's guilt.

Under new management, *The Monster* staggered about the country for a month or so, finishing up in a hall in Dover. Drew chattered away to the press about his love for an artists' model who had taken over Mrs Lindo's part. She would co-star with him, he said, in forthcoming productions. But for one reason or another – chiefly, difficulties in finding backers whose venture-capital amounted to anything like their stated assessment of it – none of the projects got off the ground.

Drew's alcoholism was getting worse. Unnerved by the tittle-tattle about the Reading murder, depressed by the breakdown of his plans, he began to feel persecuted. Self-pity increased his consumption of liquor, and this in turn deterred producers from engaging him, giving him further excuse for self-pity.

In the ten years between the end of the run of *The Monster* and his own end – his death ascribed to cancer, he was buried in a pauper's grave – he appeared on the stage for just a single week, playing a small part in a farce.

It is reasonable to assume that, whether he was innocent or guilty of the murder of Alfred Oliver, Philip Yale Drew must often have wished that the inquest jury's verdict had been explicit to him, marking the first stage of a journey whose destination was a gallows-shed.

A Night at the Movies

The main attraction at the Biograph Cinema, Chicago, on the sweltering-hot Sunday of 22 July 1934, was *Manhattan Melodrama*, starring Clark Gable and William Powell. The duty-versus-friendship theme of the picture had been used before, and would be used many times again, most profitably by Warner Brothers.

In the final couple of reels, a district attorney, played by the suave Powell, brought about the conviction of his friend, Gable, for murder, and then, for old times' sake, offered to arrange a sentence of life imprisonment. Needless to say, Gable's response was 'nothing doing' – he would rather go to the electric chair than spend his life behind bars – and in the closing scene he walked to the execution chamber while some of the studio musicians played, no, not chamber music, but a version of the '1812 Overture', and the rest tried to make themselves heard above the din with a tune that sounded suspiciously like 'Abide With Me'.

At half-past ten on the Sunday night, as the music on the sound-track swelled towards a crescendo, a dark-haired, slack-mouthed young man sitting in one of the back rows nudged his two female companions, indicating that he wanted to avoid the rush for the exits. Flanked by the women, the older of whom was wearing an orange-coloured skirt that was to become probably the most famous garment in the history of crime, he headed towards the foyer. Like the character on the screen – who at least knew what was in store for him – the young man was walking towards a sudden and violent death.

His name was John Herbert Dillinger.

In the Federal Bureau of Investigation's roll of infamy, he had been accorded the supreme title of Public Enemy Number One. Perhaps, to him, the FBI's accolade proved that he had 'made it'. The police and the press had created a mythical Dillinger – but, in so doing, they had made a self-fulfilling prophesy, for Dillinger had sought to live up to the myth, and once or twice had succeeded.

He was born in the mid-western city of Indianapolis in the summer of 1903, the son of a God-fearing grocer. His mother died from an apoplectic stroke when he was three, and his sister Audrey, already married at seventeen, moved back to the family home to look after him – or, as some accounts suggest, to protect him from his father, who was a strict disciplinarian. I leave it to psychologists to answer the chicken-or-egg question of whether young Dillinger, being innately rebellious, deserved the punishments meted by his father, or whether the punishments – extreme, some of them, including chaining to a bed – created resentful rebelliousness.

Whichever way round it was, by the time Dillinger was in his late teens, he had committed a number of petty offences. His father had remarried and was now running a small farm some fifteen miles from the city. Dillinger dropped out of school and, ignoring his father's wish that he should help on the farm, became an apprentice machinist. He spent most evenings in pool halls – in those days, a sure sign of a misspent youth – and at weekends played baseball: well enough, some spectators thought, for him to have taken up the game professionally. In later years, his athleticism, enabling him to jump over the counters in banks and to sprint faster than pursuers, would form part of the Dillinger mythology, exaggerated into a reputation that rivalled that of Spring-Heeled Jack.

Part of his nocturnal spare-time was spent with prostitutes – presumably ones who offered cheap rates, since there is no indication that his wages as an apprentice-machinist were greatly augmented by the proceeds of his crimes, which were hit-or-miss affairs, mostly undertaken on the spur of the moment.

In July 1923, when he was twenty, he stole a car from a parking-lot, only to abandon it a few hours later. Fearing arrest, he enlisted in the Navy, giving his real name but a false address. After six months, during which he was less often on duty than AWOL or suffering a penalty for an absence, he deserted the Navy for good and headed back to Indiana. There, he met, and casually married, a sixteen-year-old girl who admired his skill at baseball.

His membership of the local team also brought him in contact with an umpire who had recently completed a prison sentence for robbery. The umpire, Edgar Singleton, persuaded Dillinger to help him mug a shopkeeper. Easier said than done, as it transpired. The shopkeeper, despite being hit with an iron bolt and threatened with a pistol, refused to give up his takings, and Singleton and Dillinger scuttled away empty-handed. The shopkeeper was unable to describe either of his assailants, but the police received information through the underworld grapevine, and Dillinger was apprehended and quizzed. His father visited the county prosecutor, who promised that Dillinger would be treated leniently if he pleaded guilty. For once following paternal advice, Dillinger threw himself on the mercy of the Court. Unfortunately for him, he appeared before a severe judge whose idea of mercy amounted to a term of imprisonment of between ten and twenty years.

In fact, though he lost some remission because of several attempts to escape, he served a few months less than a decade. When he was paroled from the Michigan State Prison in the spring of 1933, he was versed in the theory of bank robbery. It may have occurred to him that his tutors – of whom the most influential were a handsome young psychopath named Harry Pierpont and the wise-cracking Homer Van Meter, a jack of many criminous trades – had not entirely mastered the theory, since they were all serving stiff sentences for robbing banks. Still, they had advised him on the basics, and he was grateful for that; he had assured them that once he had found his feet, he would arrange for their stretches to be minimized.

Starting in a small way – robbing shops before gravitating, but only slightly, to banks in sparsely populated communities in Indiana – Dillinger needed just three months to amass an 'escape fund'. Much of this was used to bribe the foreman of a Chicago firm that supplied barrels of thread to the shirt-making factory in the Michigan State Prison. Towards the end of September, one of the barrels, marked with a red X, contained only sufficient thread to act as packing for revolvers and ammunition.

In the afternoon of 26 September, Harry Pierpont and nine other convicts broke out of the prison.

By then, however, Dillinger was himself in custody. Acting on a tip-off from the Pinkerton Detective Agency that he was cohabiting with a whore in Dayton, Ohio, policemen of that city had arrested him and he was now in the nearby Lima Jail, awaiting trial.

Early in October, Pierpont and two other escaped prisoners repaid Dillinger's thread-barrel favour. Posing as officers from the Michigan State Prison, they entered Lima Jail, killed the sheriff, located the key to Dillinger's cell, and released him. He is reputed to have inquired: 'So what kept you?'

The four men drove to Indianapolis, where they split up for a couple of days – not because this was considered expedient in view of the police hunt, but because they felt like spending some time with their respective molls, Dillinger's being a half-breed Indian girl called, so she insisted, Billie Frechette.

The newspapers at first referred to the men as 'the

Lima mob', then as 'the terror gang'. A week after Dillinger's escape, he and his emancipators began to live up to the latter title – and brazenly to use it as a sort of abracadabra to enter premises they had cased for robbery.

Their first 'hit' was a police arsenal. Masquerading as tourists with a casual interest in police preparations to deal with the terror gang, they prevailed upon officers at the front-desk to show off the arsenal – and then, with the aid of revolvers produced from their pockets, induced the policemen to hand over an assortment of rifles, machine-guns, and branded-as-bullet-proof vests.

Thus the gang was well-stocked with weapons as it carried out a string of bank-robberies in the mid-western farming states. Some members of the gang were not merely prepared to use the guns, but only too eager to fire them: the slightest hesitation on the part of a cashier or a hasty movement by a customer was used as an excuse to 'pump lead'. Before long – within the couple of months at the end of 1933 and the first few weeks of the following year – the gentle profession of banking became a rather hazardous occupation.

Though Dillinger was only a member of the gang, not its leader, the police usually referred specifically to him, practically ignoring 'Handsome Harry' Pierpont and the rest, when talking to reporters. There were two reasons for this. The police hoped that by giving all the publicity to Dillinger – the least experienced of the gangsters – the others would be put out, and there would be dissension in the ranks. And there was the hope that Dillinger would be flattered into reckless-ness; perhaps, in performing his favourite trick of vaulting over counters, he would under-estimate the height of one and do himself an injury.

Apart from the over-publicizing of Dillinger, the police had no ideas on how to put a stop to the epidemic of robberies, with their concomitant killings and woundings. It was only by sheer chance that the whole gang was rounded up. A fire broke out in an hotel in Tuscon, Arizona, where two of the hoodlums were staying, and they offered firemen a large sum of money to rescue their belongings. Having pocketed the cash, the firemen opened the heaviest suitcase to see what made it so valuable, and found that it contained sufficient weapons to supply a small war. They informed the police, who quietly arrested the two gangsters in the house to which they had moved after the fire, and then snared the rest of the gang in a dragnet operation. The members of the terror gang were lodged in various lock-ups, the one chosen for Dillinger being the 'escape-proof' prison at Crown Point, Indiana.

On the day he arrived, the place was swarming with photographers and newsreel teams – and with local dignitaries clamouring to have their pictures taken with the celebrity. One of the snaps showed Dillinger in a dear-old-pals pose with the prosecutor who intended to send him to the electric chair.

After the picture session, Dillinger somehow contrived to get hold of a knife, a block of wood, and a tin of black shoe-polish, and with these everyday articles fashioned the semblance of a pistol, sufficiently realistic to cause divers guards to lay down their arms and unlock doors for him. Then he drove off in the sheriff's car. One cannot credit the story that he was singing, 'I'm heading for the last round-up,' as he disappeared from view, but it does seem true that he subsequently commented: 'A jail is just like a nut with a worm in it. The worm can always get out.' And he certainly wrote to his sister Audrey about the exploit:

Dear Sis,

I thought I would write a few lines and let you know I am still perculating. Don't worry about me honey, for that won't help any, and besides I am having a lot of fun .... I see that Deputy Blunk says I had a real forty five thats just a lot of hooey to cover up because they don't like to admit that I locked eight deputys and a dozen trustys up with my wooden gun before I got my hands on the two machineguns and you should have seen their faces. Ha! Ha! Ha! .... Now honey if any of you need any thing I won't forgive you if you don't let me know. I got shot a week ago but I am all right now, just a little sore .... Lots of love from Johnnie

Following his departure from Crown Point, he joined another gang, which numbered among its members Homer Van Meter, from whom he had learnt some of the rudiments of bank-robbery when they were convicts in the Michigan State Prison, and a homicidal lunatic who, though baptized Lester Gillis, preferred to be known as Baby Face Nelson.

But now Dillinger was being sought by the Federal Bureau of Investigation – particularly by a Special Squad, with headquarters in Chicago, that had been set up by the FBI's director, J. Edgar Hoover, to combat the mid-western crime-wave. The squad was led by a diminutive, squeaky-voiced agent named Melvin Purvis.

In April 1934, Purvis received a tip-off that Dillinger and others of the gang were staying at the Little Bohemia Lodge, a holiday chalet in the woods of northern Wisconcin, not far from the Canadian border. On the night of Sunday, the 22nd, dozens of agents converged on the lodge. It appears that some of them were as trigger-happy as the gangsters. When three male dinner-customers emerged from Little Bohemia and started towards their car, a volley of shots rang out; one of the men was killed instantly, and his companions fell to the ground, both badly injured.

Rudely awaken by the noise, Baby Face Nelson

burst out of the cabin he was sharing with his wife, and galloped off into the woods, firing at anything that moved, which included a flock of wild geese whose sleep had also been interrupted. The FBI agents, apparently assuming that the random shots were coming from the lodge, began firing at the building. The barrage continued for the rest of the night. At dawn, Purvis and a few other intrepid agents entered the tattered wreck of Little Bohemia (which, according to a wag, was 'ever afterwards known as Littler Bohemia') and found the gang's molls, whimpering and suffering from shell-shock, in the cellar. But there was no sign of Dillinger and company, who had scampered out through a back door as soon as the shooting had started.

Not unnaturally, Purvis was embarrassed by the fiasco. And so was J. Edgar Hoover. He issued a shoot-to-kill order against Dillinger, and doubled the reward of $10,000 that was being offered by authorities in five states. Over the next month or so, several men who bore a passing resemblance to the gangster (or, at least, to his most recent photograph, for he may have undergone cosmetic surgery in a drastic attempt to disguise himself) were arrested or given the nasty shock of being fired at by bounty-hunters.

Meanwhile, Dillinger was a paying guest in a brothel a few blocks from the Chicago headquarters of the FBI. He had a replacement moll, a girl called Polly Hamilton, who had recently been divorced by a policeman.

The proprietor of the brothel, a Romanian woman who called herself Anna Sage, also had a policeman in her past. Renewing contact with him, she offered to 'set up' Dillinger if the FBI would promise to halt deportation proceedings that were in train against her. The policeman introduced her to Melvin Purvis, who straightway agreed to the tit-for-tat arrangement.

Polly Hamilton's subsequent reminiscences of Life

with Dillinger suggest that if local law enforcers had
been at all alert, Purvis could have told Mrs Sage to go
to Romania. Polly – described by one of the dozens of
reporters who did so as 'a blue-eyed girl with an off-
and-on smile' – recalled many outings with her new-
found friend:

> We went out a lot. He was crazy about movies,
> and we went to nightclubs. He looked like an
> average-businessman type, and always had plenty
> of money. That's when I first started to drink
> alcohol. Probably the first drink – or two – I ever
> had were with him. I used to order Alexanders –
> or something just as fancy. We were at the Grand
> Terrace one night and I saw people looking and
> looking at him. He saw them looking, too. You
> never saw anyone call for a bill as fast as he did.
> Why, I don't think he even waited for the change.
> We took a cab to the Loop, then got another cab
> and went to the Chez Paree.
> I got a thrill out of going around in cabs. We
> cabbed everywhere. Twice he gave me money so
> my girl-friend and I could go to the World's Fair.
> He was very good-hearted, but don't misunder-
> stand: he was no sucker. He was very conserva-
> tive for the kind of money he had. I remember I
> said I couldn't go to the beach because I didn't
> have a decent bathing-suit. He wasn't about to go
> out and buy you any fur coats, but he handed me
> a whole forty dollars and said I should go and buy
> something with it. Another time, he gave me
> money to get my teeth filled.
> Let me tell you, I was crazy about him. He had
> a marvellous personality. He really *couldn't* have
> been kind and good and do all the things he did,
> but he was kind and good to me. He had very
> good innate intelligence, and was interested in
> what was going on, and I don't mean just cops

and robbers – daily *events* is what I mean. He had a low voice, rather pleasing, and was the most terrific card-player. He was crazy about cards. We played pinochle and regular rummy – penny-ante stuff, a nickel limit. One time I wouldn't pay my card bill, and he started twisting my arm. I don't know if he was serious or not – but I paid.

He was short and stocky and *very* solid. He was broad-shouldered and had *the* most fascinating smile, especially when he was playing a joke. It was a very tricky smile. He was a good dresser, clean and neat. I didn't particularly care for his taste in suits, but he was always immaculate.

There was one song Dillinger was just crazy about, from a picture we saw with Joan Crawford at the Marbo: 'All I do is dream of you the whole night through.' He used to sing it and sing it to me. He sure could carry a tune.

Sometimes Dillinger and Polly made a foursome with Mrs Sage's son Steve and his girl-friend. On one occasion they visited the Stables, a fashionable night-club in the centre of the city, and they also went to cinemas – to the Granada, to see *Viva Villa!*, starring Wallace Beery, and to the final showing at the Marbro of *You're Telling Me*, starring W.C. Fields.

Late in the afternoon of Sunday, 22 July, Anna Sage telephoned Melvin Purvis to apprise him of the fact that Dillinger was treating her and Polly Hamilton to a night at the movies. She wasn't sure of the cinema – either the Marbro or the Biograph. As the temperature was up in the 90s, she hoped that it would be the Biograph, which was cooled by refrigeration. To make it simple for the FBI agents to identify her, she would wear a brightly-coloured skirt.

So it was that when Anna Sage, the subsequently-titled '"Lady" in "Red"', emerged from the Biograph, Purvis and the host of other agents in the street knew that the man beside her, bespectacled and wearing a boater, was John Dillinger.

In the absence of a cigar-lighting signal from Purvis – whose hands were trembling so violently that he was unable to strike the match – the ambush did not resemble its plan. While some agents waited for the signal, others, assuming that it had passed unnoticed, hurried towards Dillinger. He started to run – hunched-backed, trying to make a smaller target. He got no farther than the mouth of an alley by the cinema before several heavy-calibre bullets tore through his body. Two of the bullets – or perhaps two of the many that were poorly aimed – ricocheted and wounded pedestrians. Purvis, who had not thought to leave his jacket open, ripped the buttons off in his haste to draw the guns from his belt.

Hours later, when the relic of America's Number-One Public Enemy was lying naked in a morgue, luggage-labels tagged to the big toes, and when the last of the souvenir-hunters had dipped their hankies in the blood on the sidewalk, someone – a colour-blind Chicago policeman, according to one of the umpteen Dillinger legendists – strolled into the alley and chalked on the wall near an emergency exit from the Biograph:

> Stranger, stop and wish me well,
> Just say a prayer for my soul in Hell.
> I was a good fellow, most people said,
> Betrayed by a woman all dressed in red.

Dramatis Personae